THREE SIDES

─ OF EVERY ─

[CRISIS]

STRATEGIES TO SUSTAIN BUSINESS, MANAGE
YOUR CAREER AND TAKE CARE OF YOU

What You Nurture
WILL manifest,

Jewel
DAOT '22

JEWEL W. DANIELS

Books by Jewel W. Daniels

Growing Solopreneur Businesses through Collaboration

It Takes Tenacity: 15 Powermoves to Survive the Wilderness and Weather the Economic Storm

The Enterprising Entrepreneur

_____

To contact Jewel W. Daniels

Email: connect@jeweldaniels.net

www.jeweldaniels.net

Published by Daniels Communications Global

400 West Peachtree Street, Atlanta, GA 30308

.

First Edition, 2020

Printed in the United States

ISBN: 978-0-9749991-7-3

10 9 8 7 6 5 4 3 2 1

Library of Congress Control Number: 2020909935

Dedication

This book is dedicated to my mother Diane Yarbrough, the deceased George Yarbrough, the dad who loved me as his daughter, and the deceased Llewellyn Cornell Radford, Sr. , who gave me the greatest gift of all, our daughter Jynnah Dahrey Radford. My life is rooted in what you all did right and what we collectively learned to do better.

Acknowledgement

The two greatest loves of my life, my daughter Jynnah Radford and Mother Diane Yarbrough are the models of kindness, sacrifice, and trust, all anchored in a love I am so very blessed to receive from them every day. Every woman should have the gift of a sister-friend who accepts you as you are and helps you to become even better which I found in Tina Jaya. Rodney Baker you reflect the best of what men should be and I am thankful we have become family through the village of friends and loved ones that keep us strong. My brother Brian who took every late-night call and laughed with me during midday conversations, teaching me and calling me out when I am wrong, I love you. The Diva herself, Joann Tolbert Yancy who taught me how to stand firm and confident in my gifts. To my sorors of Delta Sigma Theta Sorority, Incorporated, there is no greater sisterhood than the bonds of love and friendship than what I have found with you.

Table Of Contents

Introduction

S everal weeks ago, we were dealing with globalization that brought competition to everyone's doorstep - both small enterprise and large corporations. Organizations were grappling with growing customer demands, expanded markets, and technology that forced us to think faster, move faster, deliver faster. Human resource professionals were managing through strategic ways to meet the needs of five generations in the workforce - something we were experiencing for the first time. And just when it seemed as if all plates were more than full, we are now faced with this, COVID-19. A global pandemic that is slowing business operations, halting some, while creating new opportunities for others.

CRISIS

A time of danger;

A time of opportunity;

What do I mean? This may seem ironic because while we face this crisis, I am reminded of the Chinese symbol that represents opposite ends of the spectrum where there is both danger and opportunity. We have been here be-fore. Here, at the dawning of a crisis that tests ability to navigate through unchartered dangerous waters, where volatility, uncertainty, complexity, and ambiguity (VUCA) are present. Yet, opportunity awaits on the other side.

Let us recall the financial crisis of 2007-08, where a depreciation in the subprime mortgage market in the United States resulted in an international banking crisis.

Millions of people watched the collapse of the investment bank Lehman Brothers on September 15, 2008, where employees sat on the steps of the building in shock. The Big 3 American automakers' financial troubles came to a head, forcing a request to Congress for an approximate $34 billion lifejacket. The ripple effect created a global economic crisis that many economists viewed as the most detrimental financial event since the Great Depression.

I remember that time well. It is when I learned the painful lesson of 80/20. In this case, 80% of my revenues came from 20% of our customer base. Ouch! At that time, my team of consultants turned to me and asked, "what are we doing to do?" I replied, "I don't know, what are we going to do?" We had a wonderful relationship where we all often joked about situations, teased each other, and just found comfort in laughter when things got tough. But this time, they turned to me again and said, "seriously, what are we going to do?" True to my character, I replied, "I am serious, what are we going to do?" At this juncture, this is the primary question we face as the World Health Organization (WHO) reports in May 2020 that the coronavirus has globally affected over four million people, painfully touching every industry in one form or another, whether it is supply and demand or revenue and resources.

For organizations, the strong spirit that birthed the enterprise you created or that placed you at the helm, requires revisiting your entrepreneurial skills and leaderful visionary gifts to sustain the business. The passion and creativity used to drive the business continuously. Truth and facts intersect where understanding is gained that explains a mountain, in its design, has both peaks and valleys that are purposeful. It represents the constant ebbs and flows of the business. It tests a person's will and business acumen in ways that reveal the best of capabilities and the weakest of links. Visionary enterprises are championed by leaders who find opportunities that propel the business to new heights through innovation. The beauty of it all is that our collective history demonstrates that the most challenging times open the doors to some of the best ideas, creative solutions, and bold moves.

There is so much that is being written on strategies to help business organizations to sustain that it made me recall the vulnerability of being a young professional with little to no resources that offered advice on how to sustain and grow a career during an economic crisis. It was puzzling. Every general has front line leaders who are responsible for managing the troops. These individuals are usually part of the senior leadership team, who now become the primary bridge between company executives and staff. These leaders have built careers with expertise in solving business problems. They are responsible for moving forward the collective strategy that will drive company initiatives, sustain revenue, reduce, and retain talent. Most importantly, they develop and implement the plan that will ready the organization for creating a "new normal." And then there is the support staff, the most extensive base that propels the organization – many of whom are seeking understanding in an uncertain future. So, tell me, what is your next move?

While you are eagerly finding ways to manage the effects of the crisis on business and career, the complexity of it all can easily cause the loss of something even more significant – YOU! Fear of the unknown with the human desire to solve problems quickly can create immense anxiety. Each day news reports on the airwaves and television screens echo repetitive questions where there are yet to be solutions. That is uncomfortable. It becomes difficult because we forget that everything is a process. Turning the heat up on a pot will get it hot faster, but quick does not mean right. The current state of affairs allows you to "look through your strings," as my grandma would say. Take care of yourself by using this season as a time of introspection, reflection, and decision-making.

The most considerable difficulty comes in the automatic shift of what was normal one day and utterly confusing and abnormal the next. Such a jolt to the system where the mind and body resist the reality of your current situation. They are desperately seeking to grab hold of the security of what was once familiar. Understandably, you may find yourself in a state of what many call the stages of SARAH:

- Shock

- Anger

- Resistance

- Acceptance

- Healing/Hope (and Help)

Nothing about this was part of your plan. The shock of the coronavirus health pandemic bringing the global economy to a screeching trickle of resources, services, and financial continuity is hard to comprehend. The complexity of how and why this occurred with no formalized answers matched with everchanging, multi-channel sources of information that has citizens social distancing and quarantined evokes feelings of anger.

This became the basis for resistance to what is now a "new normal" amid an abnormal environment. Your business, professional, and personal life will have to make space for healing so new behaviors can arise, hope for better circumstances and new opportunities become your focus. I added help to the SARAH model because failing to do so is what often causes people to get stuck. Things are different now. How the world will operate is still evolving. This evolution requires that everyone must change.

During my 25-plus years as a global leadership development expert and business consultant, one thing remains true, people change for two reasons: pain or importance. The challenge is that for many, CHANGE is a six-letter curse word. People become angry, miserable, and exhausted, fighting the tides of what is a natural part of our daily existence. This crisis will be painful for many. It can be eased by choosing to deal with it constructively to seek opportunities that can bolster your current state. Foremost, we must understand that the ability to change is essential to us all. Remember, in May 2020, WHO reported that the coronavirus had globally affected over four million people. We are as far apart now as we are close together. What we do and how we do it will forever change us as a global village of citizens weaved together by our social, economic, and political needs.

Chapter 1

Make Strategic Decisions, Not Sudden Moves

Strategy

I love the principles of chess. Get in the game quickly to position your pieces. Make short-term tactical moves. Take calculated risks that al-low you to optimize on your opponent's mistakes. Think long term to attack or defend the center. And make strategic decisions with the understanding that your first moves are critically important. There is so much wisdom in that statement. When you think about it, there are very few things in life that require an immediate reaction.

Making broad, quick gestures that are not carefully thought out has the potential to create costly, long-term effects on your organization.

Therefore, your ability to deal with a crisis first means recognizing that this is a temporary roadblock. Crises alter plans and create delays that are caused by external forces. It reminds me of the analogy shared earlier that mountains have peaks and valleys which mirrors the nature business its crescendos and decrescendos. In this season of pushing through the valley, take your hand off the panic but-ton. Yes, it can be difficult. It is an instinct for most people to fix what is broken and do it quickly. Looking back there are so many things that if I had slowed down a bit, the pain of getting to my result would have been reduced. The most significant reason for you to widen your scope and review your pace is because this is something you have never encountered before. Traditionally, businesses craft strategy based on calculated consumer behaviors and stable markets with an understanding that conditions can be volatile. For many of us who travel often, we board planes during inclement weather, knowing that the plane ride will be bumpy, but we rely on a history of safe landings. In the case of operating in this climate, creating a thorough strategic plan is key to getting through these unchartered waters and avoiding mistakes that can often be unforgiving and irreversible.

Standing at the helm of the organization will require a diverse leadership styles. Use a survival strategy is needed as you seek to seal the hemorrhaging caused by the abrupt disruption to your business operations – then move to an adaptive approach. When the cold winds blow, it causes organizations to defensively guard reductions in costs, acts to preserve capital, and restructure business portfolios according to Clair Love and Philipp Tilmanns. Caution – survival strategy is a short-term response to a critical problem that requires a long-term approach.

So, where do you begin? I remember years ago when writing my book, *It Takes Tenacity, 15 Powermoves to Survive the Wilderness* and *Weather the Economic Storm*, I shared the story of how sometimes you find lessons in the most peculiar places. When I was a young military spouse of an active-duty Army Corps of Engineer officer, I struggled to understand his love for the strict discipline, protocol, and those darn SOPs (standard operating procedures) seemed, in my mind, to stifle creativity. Then there was his desire to merge this sense of structure into our personal life, which gave me heartburn. Before making any major decision, we had to do a recon (reconnaissance) – which meant I had to do serious homework. Recon is the art of researching along with observation to gain a full understanding of your current circumstances to devise a plan on how to best move forward. Although we later divorced but remained good friends, I couldn't have predicted that those Army principles and work ethic would leave me with skills I would use in both my business and personal life. This was the beginning of my awareness and understanding that business decisions must be rooted in data that provides insight and analytics that help to anticipate future outcomes. There are various ways to approach this and leveraging your people as resources can be essential.

1

Action Employee Resource Groups (ERGs)

Before you make any significant business decision, conduct a recon scrutinizing where your organization stands and what factors are impacting your current position. One approach would be to put your ERG (employee resource group) to work with a focus on creating a strategic survival plan to sustain the business. Your employee resource group should be a cross-section of individuals from various departments throughout the company. Seek volunteers and make key selections leaning on your marketing team for creativity; sales to explain revenue gains and losses; Human Resources to define policy and laws, and the training department to identify HiPros and key contributors. If your organization does not have these groups in position, now you understand the critical role they play. ERGs should represent unique perspectives, personalities, and people who are willing to contribute openly and to innovate. They should be composed of experienced, enthusiastic staff who are committed to seeing the business through this journey. The most significant benefit of ERGs is that they become the center of engagement with your organization for interaction, innovation, and communication. Caution, this will only work if it has executive buy-in with a commitment to listen, learn, and be inclusive of your VOIC (voice of internal customer).

Similar to ERGs, in times of economic and business functional dis-course, organizations form Crisis Management Teams or smaller groups based on the size of the entity and circumstances they face. The critical role of these groups is to proactively address the organization's immediate concerns by reviewing and developing policies, liaising with stakeholders, and becoming the information source for advising all levels of the organization about factors that will impact business operations. They become the organizations advising subject matter experts(SMEs) on all matters related to the present crisis with the responsibility to develop plans and policies that affect:

- Procedures for business continuity.

- Decisions that influence employee retention and reduction.

- Policies that govern changes in working operations on-site and virtually.

- Instituting regional, national and global shifts in operations.

- Succession planning contingencies

- Communications between various departments that may include logistics, operations, human resources, training, marketing and public relations.

- Advisory for media and press management.

- COVID-19 information dissemination and crisis management, prevention, and best practices.

- Documentation of all business decisions and processes.

- Company workforce readiness.

The group should spearhead a SWOT work session that identifies the current strengths, weaknesses, opportunities, and threats that can be used as a part of your organization's CMP (crisis management plan) or BCP (business continuity plan). An essential criteria is documenting all changes adopted by the organization. It is a living organism that must remain flexible to adapt to any new dramatic changes it may encounter.

In the process of determining your next move, ask some tough questions. For example, do you need to strengthen your customer base, identify new prospects, or diversify your product or service offerings? As the crisis began to reach the shores of the Caribbean, I watched many companies in Jamaica scramble for answers. Many slashed prices, others reduced their operations, and introduced new marketing schemes. Some companies began packaging goods offered at discounted prices with a 1,2,3 step process from purchase to pick up. In the United States, there was a significant upsurge in delivery services for groceries, food from restaurants, and on-line products as well as pick up orders from stores like Home Depot. This change awakened some questions about how are organizations getting the data that drives their decision-making? This huge for several reasons. During a crisis, there is often the rise of two warring factions: generals and officers, or in other words, senior leaders, and managers. Leadership that is watching the bottom line and growing more anxious that the numbers continue to drop. They begin to feel anxiety because revenues are on a rapid decline creating a sense of urgency for immediate solutions. Rapid responses.

Quick answers. And, this fuels the need to cauterize the bleeding revenues with swift decisions. In the other camp are managers who are held responsible for bridging the gap of the organization's current state of declining revenues, changes in service or product strategy with managing processes, and people challenges to bring about results. Why are they warring factions? Because when organizations seek immediacy by making sudden moves, somewhere while trying to tame a crisis, another one is brewing because strategy gets lost.

I get it. Things are tough. Times are bad. Leadership wants answers, and they want them quickly. Managers want the same thing, but the means of getting there can often differ significantly between the two groups. The coronavirus crisis has created a situation that has forced everyone's hand. Like any crisis, when widespread sweeping changes appear it quickens the desire to solve and solve fast. In some part, I believe this has been sped up by technology. Society has become deeply rooted in a love/hate relationship with technology that speeds up productivity while requiring more of our time. We live in a world where one click, push, or turn of a button provides instantaneous results. It is the addictive consumption of wanting more that fuels our heightened expectancy of how much people produce, and it continually feeds our desire for expediency. On a late Friday night, I found myself debating this very subject with one of the brightest minds in sales and strategy I have encountered in Jamaica. I passionately made my point to Everod Wilson, who has branded his career as a critical thinker who studies how to move the needle in sales and business strategy. He offered a thoughtful and tempered response that aligned with my solution for organizations that face this quandary, "why do you have to pick one?" There is such brilliance in the simplicity of his response. We agreed that organizations must leverage talent placed into teams that can simultaneously tackle both sides of the coin, short and long-range strategy. Grabbing low hanging fruit is smart, and it produces tangible results that allow leadership to realize an increase in revenue - temporarily. Companies must prepare to face the "boom-bust" that will come with the next shift that will occur during the crisis. Customers who shelter in place, those laid off from work, and others who have reductions in pay while still working will begin to change their buying habits, causing a decline in sales. Organizations must adapt and craft long-range strategic plans that are rooted in reliable data to produce a sustainable strategy. Here are some reasons organizations need to ask tough questions and practice critical thinking that will move them pass resolutions to concrete solutions. Let us begin with, "is the product or service something that customers need?" If not, how can you reposition it to something they want?

In 1973 when Martin Cooper of Motorola placed the first mobile telephone call to his rival, Dr. Joel S. Engle of Bell Labs, the average person was pretty content with the ability to place calls from their private residence or office. Nearly ten years later, Cooper, an engineer, would see his DynaTAC 800x chunky, narrow-shaped, box-style phone that weighed just under 2 pounds and called the "brick" become available to consumers. The phone had a price tag of nearly $4,000. It allowed customers to connect without operator-directed calls over a wireless cellular network, not yet fit for the average consumer. By the early 1990s, changes in design and portability caused an uptick in interest by average consumers wanting a mobile phone for convenient usability and communication. Today, changes have now blurred the line to create a shift in the way consumers want to connect more often and the need to produce rapidly to meet supply and demand. Okay, so that is a fantastic story for the ages. However, it still holds that organizations must consider how they fulfill a want and need, where is the source of this data, and what will be done with it? This is just the beginning.

The vital role of ERGs is to help companies answer a multitude of questions like "What information is influencing strategy? "How can new information be gleaned from customers? What is the plan for passive vs. emotional buyers? Others to consider are:

- Where/How will you reach new and existing customers?

- What affiliate relationships can be cultivated to extend your company's marketability?

- What can be done differently about how your company delivers its goods or services?

- What will be your company's position in the marketplace given the global economic disruptions?

- Will your business need to change to cater to a local, national, or international audience?

- What technology resources can be used to better service your customers?

These are essential things to query now that you are in unchartered territory. Fresh, timely, accurate information is required to get the best results. Be sure to expand the list to include questions that are relevant to your industry. Then look at internal and external factors than can be done to gain a more comprehensive picture of your business operations. Look to include efforts to conduct:

- Real-time customer polling by phone, virtual events, and others to best understand how the crisis will change customer behavior.

- Review your company handbook for outdated policies and procedures.

- Evaluate your support team to access their level of productivity.

2

The Power of Crowdsourcing

Some harsh realities come with managing through a crisis. The goal is to take a wide-angled look at all factors to get the most comprehensive view possible. Depending on the culture of your organization, a broad approach that includes employee feedback could discover some good ideas. Crowdsourcing can make a company feel vulnerable as you open the door to ideas that will unveil hidden deficiencies while discovering real gems. This model of seeking feedback requires great clarity of purpose and structure for employees because it is a less intense capital investment that seeks to identify various options. While it requires a high degree of planning to channel and vet the information, it affords them opportunities to create goodwill and connectedness with the team during a sensitive time. The risks are low, and the benefits high. At the other end of the spectrum is the possible negative employee perceptions of the company's direction, and poor reactions should employees' shared ideas not be adopted. Yet, I believe Jeff Howe of Wired magazine got it right. The architecture of crowdsourcing is "getting ideas from groups of people is an excellent means of gaining participation and buy-in from some of the most creative and qualified people." One of the most masterful examples of successful crowdsourcing is Facebook's evolutionary growth.

The company made a significantly bold move in 2007 when it opened its social-networking platform to the probing eyes and ideas of external developers that brought a plethora of new applications to its doorstep. Just three years later, the company had more than 500,000 apps, including games like Zynga help bolster its position in the marketplace and push out significant players like Myspace. Now the company is a leader in the social media space, making acquisitions like WhatsApp and Instagram that now have Facebook serving nearly 3 billion users. All that from seeking input from others.

3

Reduce, Retain, Refocus

Today is a strange kind of day. The sky is filled with beautiful, white fluffy clouds against the backdrop of a joyful blue sky. Yet, the winds are bustling like there is a storm on the way. I am captivated by the sweet smell of the jasmine outside my window being carried to-and-from by the strong winds. It is so wonderful. The elegance of this gets broken by my client's heart-and-hand decision to make empathetic decisions to keep large numbers of staff until his hand becomes forced to make drastic cuts. For years I have consulted clients on decisions that would determine the trajectory of their organization. When posed with questions about staff reductions, leaders often express that it is a massive and burdensome process. Reducing staff is never comfortable, yet it is a necessary consequence of those external forces that slow and sometimes cripples business. The satisfying solution: practice authentic leadership and rolling out a comprehensive communications plan that details the company's approach.

Smaller entrepreneurial enterprises face similar challenges that have the advantage of size, they can be nimbler and quicker to respond to changes in the business environment. Traditionally, this occurs due to fewer layers of decision makers. Yet, it does not minimize the potential effects of a crisis that can bring swift and sometimes devastating effects should access to liquid capital happen, or compromised supply chain, contracts become frozen, and product orders significantly decline. Nonetheless, the goal is the same – save the company from financial distress. Just as large entities, small entrepreneurial enterprises must also be transparent and own the responsibility of collaborating with team members to work through this crisis. Smart, strategic moves at the beginning of the process will carry you through the crisis and leave you ready to pivot once the market resettles.

Knowing where to begin can be difficult. Each organization will have to factor in various aspects of its operation. Answer the 5 **W's** and the **H.**

1. **Who** will be the primary group to lead the company?

2. **What** factors are within your control, and what new opportunities exist?

3. **When** will the organization roll out its crisis strategy and business continuity plan?

4. **Where** will you seek to sustain market presence vs. dominance? Why are you taking this course of action?

5. **How** will the information be communicated to internal and external customers?

These are just beginners. Dig deeper and deeper for questions to find answers.

If you recall, I shared how my team of consultants confronted me asking "what are we going to do" in the face of our business crisis during the financial meltdown of 2007-08. The easiest answer would have been for me to make decisions with limited input from the team. But throughout my years of building my career, I had seen that before and it never made sense. How could the best decision be made without the people who are equally responsible for the company's success and sustainability? For us, our group came up with a variety of solutions where we used a tiered approach that allowed team members to have a voice in how they would stay or separate from the organization.

Team members chose to take reductions in pay, adjustments in work schedules, while others would be made redundant with career transitioning support provided to them. This is where I found an opportunity to practice authentic leadership that said I have answers, but I needed my team's brainpower to uncover the best solutions.

It was a chance to implement what was the primary practice of our business, what we spent years developing and instilling in the minds of thousands of people. Our strategic first moves would speak loudly and profoundly about our company's brand of collaborative and consultative leadership.

Your job as the leader of the organization is, to be honest about the status of the organization and the direction it will pursue

In doing so, leaders can find the hidden opportunities that instill faith and respect in the business. One of the best examples is Marriott International's CEO Arne Sorenson delivering a tough and candid state of the business video message to employees where he described the coronavirus crisis as more severe for the hotel chain than the Great Depression and World War II. He was transparent when sharing that "COVID-19 is like nothing we've ever seen before" resulting in an effect on the business that was more damaging that than the worst quarter the hotel had ever experienced. This is due to hotel and event cancellations and an extreme drop in global reservations.

From authentic leadership to a comprehensive communications plan, Marriott froze hiring except for a limited number of mission-critical positions; cut executive team salaries by 50 percent and furloughed employees for as much as 90 days. All tough decisions, but strategically calculated to ensure a balanced approach that touched everyone in the company; yet, allowed it to remain operational to achieve key objectives.

I love the initiative Square took to refund all software subscription fees during March as well as Salesforce which made its Quip platform free to customers and not-for-profit organizations to help with the teleworking mandates. The later helped small businesses transition team members from working at their physical location to working virtually. Look for similar opportunities within your partnership portfolio and consider how your company may ease the burden of its customers. You see, sudden moves will not allow you to get a full understanding of what options are available. Strategic moves will. These two often get overlooked.

In times of crisis, things change rapidly so follow government social media channels and websites. It is vital to keep abreast of changing government regulations that may impact your business operations, or there may be a gem of information in the midst. The government of Jamaica was been dealing with a longstanding problem of water supply problem to various communities. The COVID-19 crisis placed an even greater spotlight on the matter as more people shelter at home, creating a higher demand for water. This opened the door opened of opportunity to award private contracts for water delivery.

Reach out to your business' three best friends: banker, accountant, and attorney. Most financial institutions make access to capital easier through loans with reduced interest rates. For existing loans seek to renegotiate terms. In the United States, small business to big business financial assistance programs have been created with bank lending to help to ease faster access to money amid interest rates that have fallen as low as 1%.

Tumultuous circumstances require strategic and timely decisions that will ease financial pressures, reduce costs, retain people, and reach objectives. Leaders must also work to enable the continuity of production, meet customer needs, and maintain profitability. In such times that downsizing becomes inevitable, just be sure to make surgical cuts. Retain, realign, reduce staff involves taking the necessary steps to determine what percentage of your staff will compose your critical action team to lead the organization through the crisis. There will still be critical roles within the organization like sales, finance, and operations that must remain. These adjustments may result in a reduction in hours or transitioning team members to contractors to ensure business continuity and survival.

Additionally, efforts will need to be made to realign responsibilities that can be temporarily combined into one position or decide who can serve in a different capacity. Separating employees is difficult. Staggered layoffs or singular company-wide reductions are made based on the vitality of the business against tumultuous headwinds. The paramount role the Human Resources (HR) team will play is to develop various options for consideration. In some cases, employees can be allowed to select which suits them best.
It fosters transparency, collaboration, care, and ownership for affected employees. Taking such a risk just might surprise you!

It is imperative that human resource directors to be a part of the executive leadership team at all times of the organization's operation. There is a beautiful Jamaican saying, "prevention is better than cure." Too often, HR is called upon to fix problems that are preventable if they have a seat at the decision-making table. There are various factors considered when making decisions for redundancy, retention, and cutting staff. Organizations should "think with the end in mind," as Stephen Covey would say to envision the type of talent needed to propel it through the crisis and onto the next plateau. Therefore, everything needs to be considered: employees with chronic performance issues, non-performers with long tenure to hi-potentials, and opportunities to realign teams. Human resource professionals must look amongst their arsenal of choices to determine the best options for employees that will ultimately leave the organization in good working order. Those may include:

ACTION	BENEFIT
Reduce work schedules in areas that exceed the capacity	Staff cost savings
Staff reduction, redundancy	Staff cost savings
Executive and C-Suite salary reductions	Cost-savings
Rotate and stagger shifts/ schedules	Save jobs
Virtual work options	Job retention/business continuity
Temporary pay reductions	Sustain employment
Sliding scale reducing high to mid-salaried employees	Job retention
Onsite healthcare (nurse, counseling)	Early detection and coping support
Hazard duty pay (factories, plants, close-quarter situations)	Employee retention and business continuity
Unpaid leave/ Employee "sabbatical"	Avoid layoffs
Freeze, salary-increase, and bonuses	Avoid layoffs
Sick leave, vacation benefits usage	Employee support and retention
Flextime and vacation time	Employee retention
COVID-19 paid time off	Care for symptomatic employees
Short-term disability and FMLA usage	Employee support and retention
Expand health services (mental wellbeing, coaching, etc.)	Employee support and retention
Hazard/quarantine pay (quarter to half of the monthly wages)	Employee support and retention
Employee Assistance Programs (EAPs)	Employee support and retention
Community partners (childcare centers, accelerated banking)	Employee support and retention
Realignment of workspace	Safe social distancing

When tough decisions need to be made, employees want to see, not just hear, that there will be burden-sharing taking place throughout the organization. When you get to a juncture that requires reductions in your workforce to save jobs, ensure that it is reflective at the highest levels of the organization. Senior leaders and C-suite executives must openly share decisions that are just as significant for these roles, with the CEO leading by example to take the most significant cut in salary.

Employers will need to undertake a variety of options based on a cross-section of factors with consideration given to balance sheets, consumer needs, brand positioning, and employee wellbeing. Companies like CVS have increased benefits like an additional 14 days sick leave pay for those testing positive with COVID-19, bonuses, and day-care benefits as a means of retaining employees working during the pandemic. While some organizations HR departments will be at the forefront of managing difficult staff reduction decisions, retention, and realignment actions, there will be a swell in customer demand for other industries. Rapid hiring for temporary and permanent positions will be necessary for areas like healthcare, grocery stores, online companies like Amazon is adding 100,000 employees in shipping and delivery services, and technology. Therefore, the right measures will need to be put in place to balance recruiting that will allow the organization to scale effectively to ensure rapid, yet competent hires. The crisis has helped to reveal future state processes that will see greater and broader use of technology across industries, which would be an incredibly useful recruiting tool. To accelerate recruiting cycles, organizations should consider focused efforts that include:

- Online applicant platforms
- Videoconferencing interviews
- Candidate pools

These efforts are successful with a robust onboarding and orientation process that acclimates new employees and helps them to be well-prepared to quickly get up to speed in meeting production and performance goals. The staff that remains works to meet current demands and to stay competitive. Shifts in the business climate will require the business to be ready to ramp up when an economic turnover occurs. Sustaining quality, maintaining the product, and service value are important factors in preserving your organization's reputation.

4

Communicate Widely, Deeply and Often

It may seem strange that communication gets such attention. However, in my 25 years as a leadership development expert, it remains among the top requested areas of soft skills training. People often ask me why is this the case?

The answer is we are all human beings looking through a lens-shaped by how we individually would like to see things happen. At some juncture, we meet at an intersection where our opinions do not align, and this causes discourse. In a crisis, the most critical thing that a business must do is to increase communication widely and deeply. This most certainly is not the time to hide the facts. Transparency is crucial for your clients as well as the employees because they are your front-line ambassadors who connect daily with your customers. Doing anything less will create more havoc within your organization as well as with your external environment because poor crisis communications will undermine all your efforts to manage the situation effectively. It can also cause lack of trust, low morale, and poor customer relations which can undoubtedly compound the issues.

What is essential in this process is making a mind shift that moves the heaviness of the crisis to share both the reality and more positive sides of the situation. Emotional intelligence is vital as leaders must extend a high level of understanding and empathy toward employees whose futures are uncertain whether there is a current continuity to their work or those whose hours and jobs may get cut. Prepare for a wide range of reactions from team members, remaining acutely sensitive to the situation and reinforce that you are all a part of the journey. Have a solid game plan that also includes talking to employees about their financial situation by having a financial adviser on hand, perhaps from your company's banking institution, that can provide some guidance. People can often take what you tell them; but it is the manner in how it is communicated that causes acceptance or rejection.

Transparency can often be difficult for organizations and their leadership. Many leaders have been taught to believe that if they admit the company is facing a difficult time, it will scare employees. The truth is that they are already frightened by the situation, so providing them with limited information will cause them to fill in the gaps with details that may not be factual. The focus should be on finding comfort with the fact that everyone is going through this global pandemic. There is not one organization that is going untouched by the current situation. The reality is that every sector of the economy is getting struck by the changes in consumer behavior. Each day people awaken to news about the state of the economy. Be specific with your information, emphasizing that the company will explore every effort to continue productivity, retain jobs, and provide support in areas for those who may be separated from the organization. Employees want honesty, and they want to see that your company is trying to assist them through these difficult times, even if it is not financial. Avoid making grossly vague statements like "we will look out for our staff first." The immediate thought for staff members will be what does that mean? Be honest about the company's financial state and truthful about the status of their jobs. Tell them specifically what are your priorities which may be to make swift adjustments to your production and make changes that reduce costs. If so, say that exactly.

Determine how you will manage internal and external communications. Develop plans, procedures, and use your team to examine current conditions and plan beyond the crisis.

Crisis command – this is the designated central location for all. Some actions to consider are:

- Incoming and outgoing communications. It serves as the common area for tracking critical information.

- Ownership – You must decide who will be who responsible for the communications plan . Based on the size and needs of your organization, a crisis management consultant may be necessary. If not, create a designated team that will dissect the program to create specific, measurable, attainable, realistic and time-bound (S.M.A.R.T) goals that are assigned to team members with the appropriate skills, will and desire.

- Medium – diversify the modes of communicating that include the classic emails, collaboration tools like Trello and Google Docs while including town halls, direct communication as well as video or audio-conferencing platforms (e.g. Go-to-Meeting, Microsoft Teams, Skype, Zoom, and others). These keep employees connected for virtual meetings and allow clients to attend on-line training sessions, when available.

One of the most important things your company can do is to be proactive. Do not wait for employees to ask questions to avoid negative thoughts and behaviors that weaken trust and productivity. Additionally, given the degree of severity of the situation that fosters feelings of anxiety, fear, and other emotions, commit to finding ways to engage team members in productive and fun ways. It is important to keep spirits high, and minds focused on the positive aspects taking place in the organization. Create unique ways to greet everyone like the "Wakanda Forever" salute from the Black Panther move or the "Vulcan Salute – Live Long and Prosper".

5

Training and Development

Training is an extension of human resources that organizations often overlook until it is needed. In cases where technical skills are required, training is a regular part of strategic initiatives. Now is the time to expand training opportunities, particularly for frontline leaders, supervisors as well as managers who will assist with corona-virus containment and other crises. Security, essential contractors, and maintenance teams also need to be included in training initiatives.

It is imperative to provide proper training for team members who will have the responsibility of engaging directly with employees to address their immediate concerns and fulfill employee needs.

These individuals will need to be thoroughly knowledgeable in the following areas:

- Local labor laws.

- Company policies for virus management and prevention measures.

- Workplace health management criteria.

- On-site and off-site hygiene practices.

- New security standards and practices

- Violation consequences

It is imperative to make the development of soft skills a critical part of the company's overall strategic plan. Now, is when leaders in the organization must practice the highest level of emotional intelligence, skillful communication, team collaboration, strategic decision making, critical thinking and crisis management, conflict resolution, coaching, and personal accountability. Whew! What a list. These are skills that are not automatically practiced by individuals and they do not come naturally for all. They are essential to the productive performance of employees, no matter what title an individual holds. There are often challenges in getting companies to see why soft skills are important because it is not a tangible product. However, it is an essential component of employee development because it is felt daily from person to person in the organization.

People who get promoted to leadership roles this does not automatically come as part of their skill set. This circumstance makes a point of why organizations must have employee development programs as a regular part of their strategic plan. It is in times of crisis that well-trained employees held accountable to performance review standards will possess the instinctual ability to draw upon those resources. Those skills should be used to help move the organization throughout and beyond a crisis. Should it be the case that your organization does not have an active employee development program in place, this crisis will demonstrate who needs skills development as well as who is successfully practicing the tools that they have learned.

Organizations that invest in employee development programs reap the benefits of team members ready to take action. Poor execution of training is the fault of performance goals not being linked to formal follow up. Also, a lack of goal setting and clearly define objectives woven into outlined expectations for employee performance. When there is a failure by employees and supervisors to conduct regular check-ins there is no room to provide feedback on milestones achieved, corrections needed or to give accolades.

As the organization moves forward, leaders must remember that this is new to everyone; therefore, communication must be wide and deep. When leadership has long gaps in between communication, feelings of anxiety and fear accelerate and find their way back into the minds and hearts of your team members, which will always cause confusion and reductions in productivity. Utilize multi-channel communication that includes everything from email to social media. Keep in mind the various demographic groups that exist within your organization. A study says that 30% of Gen Z use social media as their primary information resource. It is important for all the forward-facing team members, in particular, to maintain a positive attitude and consistently remind yourself that this is new. While you are walking in the unknown cope by dealing with problems openly and be willing and ready to learn.

This is a complicated situation. Organizations should seek to simplify the process as much as possible. Eliminate unnecessary layers that will deter from your primary goals and keep the main thing the main thing. Always prioritize short and long-term objectives that measure against your highest priorities. We have discussed a lot about making strategic decisions and not making sudden moves, an effort that is also relevant to leaders in the company. Some of the most challenging emotions to manage during the crisis is the inability to control things and utilizing skills, knowledge, techniques, and resources that once worked in your favor. This global health pandemic has leveled the playing field in a way most of us have never seen before. It has taken away the wealthy peoples' ability to utilize money to get what is desired and stymied the most talented individuals' technique for using his or her unique assets to get things done. Every single person, with no regard for economic, social, or political status, has been affected in a way that causes tremendous feelings of loss of control. Consider the thought that when you seek out the negativity, that is what you will find. It is a waste of time to revel in the most extreme adverse circumstances that exist because there are no solutions to be found in that situation. Instead, the fearless innovation that called your inner entrepreneur out of its restful sleep to bring your idea to fruition has to be reactivated. The drive to accomplish a particular level of academic success or technical expertise such that it would be set apart from the rest - that energy must be re-energized. A crisis comes along to test the greatest of will. Defeat shows up when you give up. What has guided me throughout my career is the belief that failure is not an option. If I experience a temporary setback, my strategy is to analyze the situation to ask myself, "was I properly prepared for the opportunity that I sought?" Was the timing right for the objective I was trying to achieve?

Did I make every effort to get the knowledge and support necessary to be sure I was capable? Or, was this a chance to sow seeds that could be harvested later? Did I overextend myself, that when faced with difficulty, I failed to prepare? Whatever the answers, use the experience to propel yourself. That is why strategy always wins against a sudden move.

"Jumping at several small opportunities may get us there more quickly than waiting for one big one to come along. ."

– Hugh Allen

Chapter 2

From Blue Oceans to Fast Seconds

The Art of Discovering New Business Opportunities

I have always been a rebel. In business, I believe you should always learn the rules of the game, then change them to work in your favor. Yes, this situation was unforeseen for many people. And, there is nothing comfortable about being seated amid a crisis. Yet, if we are realistic about the very nature of business in disruptive. It has its ebbs and flows and is invulnerable to unknown shifts to its external environment. In this case, COVID-19 has had a dramatic impact on various industries and people whether it be international travel, hospitality health care, food, manufacturing, logistics-basically every facet of business has been touched.

There is surely a degree of discomfort when facing this situation. What is most important is that you do not panic or have an abrupt, sudden response that could exacerbate the situation. When faced with a crisis, the impulse is to find a solution quickly. Instead, leaders must strengthen sensing skills, and business acumen gained, spending adequate time to assess, then situation, the act. This is the crossroads where innovation and ingenuity meet with collaboration and a determined spirit to find unique ways to keep the wheels of commerce moving. This is when becoming a game changer is linked to your ability to thrive.

1

Adapt and Reshape Your Circumstances

In times like this I get excited. That is from a business perspective. Historically, the level of creativity heightens during the times of most difficulty, and the environment gives birth to some of the most innovative game changers of that period. This is when the truly gifted and talented entrepreneurs rise to the top. This is when the greatest of minds who are peddling through the channels of disruption find their way to innovation. It is the sweet spot of business that proves just how incredible the human spirit is when tested. On the other side of COVID-19, like with many other crises, we will find new business leaders that will emerge, salespeople who take downturns in markets as opportunities to find new solutions for generating revenue. It is that amazing place where most people see nothing but disaster while the select few find the hidden jewels of opportunities that are all around us. I am nearly sure that at this point, you probably feel like I sound like an idealist or the most optimistic person that always sees the glass as half full. Well, you're right about the second part of that thinking. I am quite aware of the challenges that are before us because I have experienced them quite intimately as an entrepreneur. I know that there are thousands of communities and economic markets that are challenged to find their way out of the darkness. That very darkness reminds me of a good friend Renee Godefroy. He once told me that when he was a small child growing up in his Haitian village one of his inspiring memories was that when he was surrounded by darkness it was broken by the stars in the sky. He found it fascinating that while the ground was dark, the sky could be bright and shiny with stars that appeared to shine their brightest on the darkest of nights.

His stories and personal journey are one of many guideposts presented to remind us that staying the course can bring great rewards. Renee grew up in a poverty-stricken village, where he as a small child, was often teased and ridiculed because he had a frail body structure. He often described himself as having a swollen tummy due to lack of food and weakness in his bones that caused him some difficulty to walk at times. The locals in his community called him kokobay, a Creole word that means crippled. Many predicted that his weak, feeble body would not allow him to live much less reach adulthood. While most predicted his life would be filled with adversity, and would be short in length, Rene found his way to the United States where he worked for years as a doorman in Atlanta, Georgia. He used his time wisely learning English and asking every notable individual he could get a chance to speak to what was their secret sauce to success. He took their words seriously, crafting them into his own personal action plan that would eventually see him become a renowned speaker and author. In his book *No Condition Is Permanent*, he speaks about the will to overcome extreme difficulty to take control of life so that you reap the rewards that only YOU have the ability to grasp. The power to achieve, despite your personal wilderness or economic storm requires tenacity. A relentless will to meet the challenges of this crisis head on or as I say stand before the 900-pound rock in front of you and decide how you will get around it, take a rope and climb it or make a path that takes you through it. That is how you will find the new direction for your organization. This global pandemic presents a challenge to the most formidable business leaders in the world. It demands that you remain laser focused on your vision while taking the pulse of business measuring shifts in the wind to understand how to become agile so that you are able to adjust your sails.

The current state of affairs needs flexibility that can be leveraged by utilizing a shaping strategy that adopts short or continual planning cycles. The fluidity of this process gives organizations a chance to action a portfolio of experiments that climbs over boundaries to become inclusive of an ecosystem that draws in customers, suppliers, and perhaps complementors. New markets are discovered, business standards are elevated, technology platforms created, and business practices expanded. Internet software companies are known for this practice much like the story of Facebook inviting developers to help shape its platform of services which burst open the door to new communities of thought, innovation, and strategic business partnerships. This will be the new normal of business. Now, you have to decide how to get there?

Every organization's journey is different. It is the middle of the week boasting a lovely day outside because the clouds are sparse, the wind is calm, and the ocean is an enticing color of blue. That wide open, big body of blue ocean is the backdrop of a term coined by Chan Kim and Renee Mauborgne that describes a strategic approach where business seek fresh, new, and yet to be discovered areas of opportunity that will help propel them to new heights. Opportunists

bask in ways to create new products or services in a particular
industry, where market domination can be gained coupled with
good scalability and strong revenue. These pioneering innovators
become known as market disruptors because they learned the rules
of the game and then mastered them in a way that drastically caused
a change in their industry. I love it! One good example of a market
disruptor is the value innovation strategic approach undertaken by
Vistaprint, where the company would develop proprietary software
and production technology to achieve its goal of creating a shared
mass customization platform (MCP). This allowed the company to
become market dominator for years in print marketing, especially
for small and midsize companies. A more recent example is the
brainchild of Uber founders Travis Kalanick and Garrett Camp
whose concept of being able to call for a taxi from your phone
erupted on a cold Winter night in 2008 when they could not get
a ride while in Paris. That frustration led to innovation that was
born during the time period of the economic fallout from the
mortgage crisis. The result, a smart phone application that is now
used globally to call for rides and even deliver food. Years later,
Uber would expand its portfolio to launch Uber Eats. The company
could arguably be considered to have entered the highly competitive
market called red oceans. If you love the blood sport of competition
where companies fight to be the best amongst all industries within
a global market space, welcome to red ocean territory. It is a push
and shove, constant effort to outdo and outpace business rivals in
nothing less than a cutthroat race to cross and win at the finish line.
The subsidiary Uber Eats was introduced in 2014 to battle in the
food delivery market with existing competitor GrubHub, the market
leader with over $7 billion in earnings. Also occupying market space
is Door Dash, Post-mates, and Caviar. Uber Easts has strong market
share but continues to spend largely in a market where it struggles to
become profitable.

Red Ocean Strategy	Blue Ocean Strategy
Compete in existing market space.	Create uncontested market space.
Beat the competition.	Make the competition irrelevant.
Exploit existing demand.	Create and capture new demand.
Make the value-cost trade off.	Break the value-cost trade-off.
Align the whole system of a company's activities with its strategic choice of differentiation or low cost.	Align the whole system of a firm's activities in pursuit of differentiation and low cost.

Theses strategic approaches are just the beginning of what can prove to be an exciting quest to an unknown, yet profitable destination. They are offered as examples of two opposite ways to review what lies on the horizon in this crisis. There is space to be made for the evolution of organizations that must find new ways to exist. Another pathway could be through pursuit of submarkets behind blue ocean dominators or what is known as a fast second position. This is a parallel side road approach that Constantinos Markides and Paul Geroski discovered has its benefits. For example, the entry of Lyft into the personal passenger ride-sharing market behind Uber demonstrates how a company found success after the path had been paved by a market dominator. During times of crisis, fast-second affords businesses the opportunity to watch, learn, calculate, and then move. This can be favorable as it provides time to improve products, raise capital, strengthen distribution channels, and enhance innovation by learning the lessons of the first entrant. Companies like Google, that is now the premier search engine, came along later into its respective industry. Southwest, a low-cost airline, made a masterful move to control surging fuel costs by entering into long-term contracts which helped it to become a market leader. Great examples of lessons learned by being in the second seat.

A bit of Caution. Pay attention to the ease with which you seek out the low hanging fruit. The strategies that are easiest for you to execute are those that look and feel familiar to things of the past. However, they may not be sustainable for this current environment. Dominance achieved in a particular industry can be achieved by observing as a follower where you learn how to become the leader. To lead the pack, organizations will have to try and test, test and try new innovations. The goal is to examine the company's ability to break new ground, abandon old habits that will not work in the evolving crisis climate. Instead, push the boundaries to help foster a new organizational dynamic of inventiveness, company adaptability and enhanced employee performance. The new strategy should uniquely position you to form stability through:

$$\text{Operational Effectiveness} + \text{Measured Improvement} = \text{Business Continuity}$$

2

Quick Wins

As you move forward, companies should assess all means at their disposal to generate revenue. This can include company specialty products, distribution, and supply chains as well as intangible assets. Make every effort to undercover hidden revenue that would previously not have been considered absent the current situation. After taking inventory of these of these areas, here are some mid-level strategic moves to consider:

- New product offering – Isinnova, an Italian start-up offering earthquake sensors and bicycles before COVID-19 adjusted their 3-D printers to manufacture medical valves for ventilator machines.

- New client service – our company Daniels Communications Limited started offerings COVID-19 Coaching Conversations for employees of existing clients experiencing difficultly managing stress and workplace transition.

- Change mode of product delivery – regional pop-up food shops and home deliveries of groceries have become the norm for bringing goods to consumers.

- Explore partnership opportunities – UK-based Native Antigen Company (NAC) and Oxford Genetics (OXGENE) created a strategic partnership to increase production of COVID-19 antigen.

- Revisit company offerings – Portland, Oregon's Shine Distillery & Grill switched from being a micro-distillery and restaurant to selling private label sanitizer.

- Extend your geographical reach – become a history-maker like Jamaica-based Quality Incorporations VII Ltd that became the country's first toilet paper manufacturer to ship to the United States amid shortages due to increased purchases brought on by the coronavirus.

- Explore a new customer base – several food distribution companies that once relied heavily on the retail market made a shift to focus sales activities toward the consumer market.

- Consider a different delivery platform – several entities

moved their services to online platforms to reach customers sheltering at home during the crisis.

- Plan for the bounce back – capture all critical information that can be used for your post-COVID-19 business strategy.

- Chart new territory – partner with chambers of commerce, speakers bureaus, industry associations and similar organizations to programs and activities to fulfill community-based initiatives.

3

Seeing beyond the invisible boundary

I have yet to find someone who has said this crisis has been easy for them. Even the greatest of introverts, some of whom are my colleagues and family members, have admitted that coping with this global pandemic has been difficult. Our organization is no different. As a leadership development company, we face the challenge of trying to find ways to remain significant and present for our client. This crisis paved a way for us to reapproach offering online training which we sought to provide several years ago in Jamaica when first launching the Caribbean arm of our company. However, the market was not quite ready for it. Many of our clients had not come to embrace the use of virtual technology as a regular part of how they conducted business. Now, things have changed making space for a shift in our business model that allows clients to engage in learning, using our on-line platform.

During this difficult time, the most significant level of support we have been able to provide is COVID-19 coaching conversations.

Get ready for this part. We did it at no cost. In the introduction of my book, I shared with you that the only way that we were going to get through this crisis successfully is if we do it together. That also means looking at how you contribute in a way that show your organization is equipped to be an authentic strategic partner and good corporate citizen. This was the result of realizing that several employees in various organizations were truly struggling with the most basic ways to adjust in this new environment. Our solution was to offer coaching sessions for our clients' employees giving them a safe place to unpack a lot of the anxiety that was causing them to lose focus while at work. For us, this was not about offering absolute solutions because that is not what coaching does. It was a concerted effort to use the skills that we have to help walk alongside people who are struggling. It also helped to keep our promise to be the strategic partner our clients needed. I can hear your thoughts; how do you monetize this during a crisis?

One of the most significant lessons I have learned as an entrepreneur is that relationships are the currency of business. This lesson began from my relationship with one of my mentors the master of networking business icon and Author George Fraser, Founder of the Power Networking Conference. It was through his teaching and career that I came to understand creating connections with people is one of the most impactful actions one can take in this lifetime. This is something that comes naturally to me because of my love for people paired with my love to help develop people to become their best selves. Once I became an entrepreneur, I understood it more deeply. Practicing an authentic interest in people that is matched with a constant pursuit of excellence yields strong relationships. It is not as the common expression says, "it's all about who you know". Well, I know Oprah Winfrey, but she doesn't know me. How does that work in my favor? Truly, it is the relationships that we form that sustain us through times of difficulties and assist us in times of plenty that allow us to flourish. This is exactly how we were able to provide a service to our client at no cost. It also was the door that lead us to contracts with new clients who were referred to us because of our commitment to our existing customers. There are so many great things that are hidden all around which you will discover through individual effort and those that will be revealed to you by others. The principles of developing authentic relationships and giving have always yielded high returns.

The reality remains that every entity faces a different set of circumstances that bare down on the organization based on its unique position in the marketplace. The common denominator is unforeseen opportunities in the midst of this storm. Most companies find that it is inevitable to discount goods and services. In several cases it became the entry into a new way of reaching a customer base that was once a secondary market. This created strong benefits for Jamaica's Caribbean Producers of Jamaica (CPJ), once the company started bundling food products to create "bucket" sales offered directly to the consumer. Prior to COVID-19, the company primarily sold to retail outlets and were a major distributor to the tourism and hospitality industry on the island until the resorts began to close their doors as bookings declined due to an increase in coronavirus cases and government social distancing initiatives. This was a boost to the company's sales which was supported on the back end by managing their logistics and working closely with suppliers. Remember, your external partners are also facing their own set of challenges to meet fluctuating demand and even payroll, so including them in your strategic goals will be critical to predicting sales. In an effort to generate revenue quickly, discounting is one of the easiest low hanging fruits to leverage. It is a good strategy for the here and now; however, organizations must be forward thinking to create a plan for a drop in volume sales when a lag occurs in consumer purchasing. When done right, it can create a new stream of income should long term, measured practices be adopted.

Across the globe, companies are exploring a multitude of options.

Product discounts – normally this is done to promote store traffic, but these are different times. The focus is to generate sales that bring immediate revenue into the business that fits the budgets of customers who are managing their expenses due to changes in their work conditions. It helps with cashflow, draws in existing customers while attracting new ones, even if for a short term. A smart approach can be leveraged for longer term sustainable benefits and can earn loyal customers.

Co-marketing campaigns – collaborate with a business that offers a complementary service or product to help generate income and acquire new customers.

Incentive offerings – provide customers with a discount card for specific amounts of volume purchases that can be used within a given time period. This shows appreciation and helps to spur purchases made in the near future.

Reduce oversupply – moving inventory will become more challenging for non-essential retail as demand declines. Host special discount sales to generate revenue by moving deadstock or under-performers. Use the ABC analysis method to prioritize items that are most valuable, A-grade; offer a moderate return, B-grade; low-value. C-grade products that collectively represent loads of transactions but do not generate much when they stand on their own.

Local business collaborative – create or participate in a consortium of small local, community-based businesses that strategize customer offerings that range from pre-order of products to bulk purchase incentives.

Reduce expenses to recapture cash. In a crisis environment, having access to liquid capital is king. There are various methods to gain access to much needed cash.

- Critical mass – sell low performers to liquidation retailers to negate a cash crunch. This can be a hard decision and should be pursued when it is absolutely necessary.

- Reduce the payment window to suppliers, vendors and contractors to hold onto working capital. Keep it ethical by openly communicating with external partners about timelines for payment, and work to create mutually acceptable terms. Once the organization is operating in the "new normal" these are relationships that you will need again so they must be protected.

- Temporary halts – this should be placed on standard, rotating orders with suppliers if a decline occurs in customer demand exists. Again, open communication is critical to sustaining the business relationship and co-creating a workable plan.

- Government programs – a number of countries are offering a wide range of financial tools to help business. Many of these include low interest loans, grants, delayed tax payments and some exemptions. The goal is to access reasonably priced debt and equity during crisis times and delay some large financial obligations that will allow for cash flow to keep operations afloat.

There are changes to come for everyone.

4

Some hard truths

This health pandemic has revealed some harsh realities about the way we are living. The world has come to see that in some of the richest countries people are living 30 days away from not having enough money to pay bills and buy groceries. The naked truth has seen several large organizations hemorrhaging revenue and some looking to permanently close stores predicting an inability to survive in the wave of exorbitant declines in revenue. Some of the hardest hit industries like airlines, entertainment, food, fuel and the hospitality industry will have to revisit their business models as consumer behavior means wearing masks, social distancing, and staying at home. Changes will need to be made for brick and mortar stores that rely on large volumes of instore visits, face-to-face meetings will need to adjust to a new medium for connecting amongst others.

It is time to go back to school. Not literally, but figuratively in that as heads of the organization swimming in unknown, choppy and dangerous water, it is imperative that minds be turned to learning. Information has to be gained from various locations where studying the survivors of past economic crises and those who emerged as innovators. I offer the examples of blue oceans verses red, and fast seconds as ways to lift strategic thinking that works toward thrival – not just survival. During this period of uncertainty, this is about tenacity and grit!

5

Business Growth Areas

These are industries that will more than likely see an increase in customers and market share.

Delivery Food Service

Take the food service industry for example where restaurants are closed or having to find ways to serve fewer customers due to social distancing directives and quite honestly, customers fears of being in large crowds of people who may have the coronavirus. Food delivery service should be a strong consideration for restaurants. Shelter-in-place orders have resulted in an uptick in demand for delivery services, particularly for food and groceries. However, the normal process of phone orders may prove challenging as the volume may be quite higher. This is a great time to take advantage of tech savvy Millennials who are most comfortable in the in the world of utilizing all things online or via Apps on phones. Explore ways to create your own App by using cost-friendly professionals like those found on Fiverr.

Grocery Stores

The vital epicenter of needs for every person, grocery stores have seen increased sales due to customers stocking up on food to eat at home in part due to the closure of many restaurants. According to that National Grocers Association, an American organization that represents independent supermarkets that " are on the front lines of emergency response both in preparation for an impending disaster and as one of the primary operations that must be up and running for a community to be able to recover after a disaster strikes." The crisis has resulted in independent grocers helping larger chains to meet demand.

Cleaning Services

The coronavirus pandemic has forever changed the way the world looks at cleaning. Creative ways to wash your hands by counting your ABCs has become normal for most people. Deep sanitizing of public transportation vehicles to brick and mortar facilities like hair salons, manufacturing plants and call centers have become mandatory. This has created a high demand for commercial cleaning services.

Drive-in Movie Theaters

While there are not a tremendous number of drive-in movie theaters around, it presents a great opportunity for people to escape the weight of shelter-at-home orders that may be lifted. The theaters provide a way to observe social distancing that cannot be found at regular theaters that require movie-goers to share small spaces and gather in common areas. Restaurants with the real estate to accommodate cars affix large screens in the parking area and deliver food to movie-goers.

Canned Food Suppliers

During a crisis one of the most immediate responses is personal survival which means food. A need to have access to nonperishable goods. This battle can be won.

As you steady your course, here are five things to consider:

1. People are craving for some normalcy to return. Help provide some of that for them. In the state of Massachusetts, at the time of writing this, restaurants and food establishments (e.g. coffee shops) are restricted to take-out and delivery only. Customers' routines are disrupted. In this situation, delivery service providers like GrubHub and UberEats are lowering the barrier for food establishments to serve off-premise customers. Level up your customer service game by having a remote/off-premise service game plan. According to McKinsey, this market has been experiencing consistent growth and this crisis will only accelerate this trend.

2. Reach out to your lenders to negotiate short-term relief. This could either be in the form of deferred payments or extended credit lines. The median small business holds 27 cash buffer days in reserve. Federal and State government agencies have announced several relief programs, which make it easier for lenders to have these conversations with small businesses. But as a small business owner, you need to be proactive in reaching out before the situation snowballs into a bigger financial challenge. Power tip: Follow your state government Twitter feed for timely relief information announcements. Also, follow NFIB to stay on top of emerging regulations that you may need to be compliant. NFIB is the voice of small business, advocating on behalf of America's small and independent business owners.

3. Reach out to your vendors to confirm supply continuity. Some of these could be small businesses as well and could be facing their own hardships. Some of them could offer

you deferred payment terms. And while you are at it, please consider doing the same for your customers if you happen to be a B2B (business-to-business)shop.

4. Discounts are a win-win. While discounts are typically used as an instrument to promote store traffic, remember that several of your customers may have had their employment hours cut and are probably facing a personal cash flow crunch. Any discounts that help customers manage their expenses better, even for a short while, is bound to earn you loyalty in the long run.

5. Pay attention to your competition – If you are good at what you do, you won't fear the competition. But don't underestimate them either. Do not feel as if you must follow in step with what they do because it may not fit your business model. Instead, look for opportunities where they lose ground or leave a territory and find the gem of an open field that awaits you.

For those that are able to survive and lift their heads above the current fray, they are likely to succeed in a greater fashion when the recovery occurs, and it will. The reason: there will be a vacuum void in the availability of goods and services that will need to be filled. There will be fewer market leaders to fill the void when demand returns. You must be among the few.

Chapter 3

IT's a New World Now

It is said that the measure of a man is revealed not in the best of times, but during the worst. Here, we are walking through the reality of volatility, uncertainty, complexity, ambiguity, (VUCA), a state of being crafted by the US Army War College. Businesses are living organisms currently seated in a position where great adaptability and repositioning is required. The differentiator will be organizations that welcome the need to be agile in a world where chaos is causing significant disruption. It is a test of leadership that navigates through what is perceived and known, to create a new vision for the future. An organization's degree of responsiveness will permanently affect the vitality and sustainability of the business. While leaders learn from the past to make transformative decisions in the present, those lessons become the basis for strategies to build a better future. This moves them from the chaotic, quantum environment which Margaret Wheatley describes as a constant state of disorder, working in the unknown to practice vision, understanding, clarity, and agility, a process defined by Bob Johansen.

This is where the uncomfortable, frustrating attributes of chaos form a different environment and where an organization's new practices become a natural process. Shifts in processes, plans, and policies are the evolutionary results of change brought on by the COVID-19 crisis environment. And, this is just the beginning of the "new" normal.

Finding new business also means considering the four-way breakaway model created by Buisson and Silberzahn. Organizations would need to address:

- How can greater value be achieved?
- How to offer a product without changing its essence?
- How to identify ways to bolster logistics, manufacturing, and the value chain to dominant the market?
- How to use technology to accelerate growth?

Welcome to the stay at the home economy! Where teleworking, video conferencing, e-commerce, and distance learning will become permanent fixtures. Data and artificial intelligence (AI), telehealth, and supply chain management will lead to innovative changes that shows Intelligent Technology (IT) is the new world order that drives business ingenuity. According to the Atlantic Council GeoTech Center, data and AI will be the most pronounced influencer in technology innovation within the next two to five years. Many of these industries intersect as a means to meet consumer supply and demand expeditiously and profitably.

Five years ago, Daimler Trucks debuted the world's first licensed 18-wheel semi-tractor trailer, The Freightliner Inspiration Truck, that could drive itself and later completed a 10,000-mile test drive in Germany. At that time, the focus was on technology that would help reduce accidents, improve fuel consumption, and safeguard the environment. Now, US-based Starsky Robotics, is looking to commercialize automated truck technology that has an on-board self-driving system paired with a remote operator to guide the vehicle (when necessary). The vehicle is patched into the company's "teleoperations" center where a remote operator monitors on-board truck cameras to assess situations that may require managing control for the self-driven vehicle. Data is studied from testing of these vehicles that will be used to haul everything from mail to medicine as an innovative approach to meet supply chain demands. I cannot imagine what my reaction will be to see a self-driving 18-wheeler rolling alongside me on the highway. It elicits all kinds of thoughts that are opposing – elimination of human capital; and objectively favorable, as one comes to understand that automation can increase productivity and accuracy, save costs, and keep people safe when used in high-risk situations. According to research, while data and IT lead innovation, it is closely followed by medical bioengineering, supply chains, and the changes in the future of work.

Tech area with the most impactful innovation in the next 2-5 years.

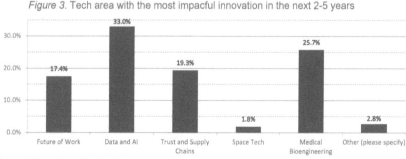

Figure 3. Tech area with the most impacful innovation in the next 2-5 years

Source: Atlantic Council's GeoTech Center

The unprecedented effect of this pandemic has created a crisis that makes it challenging to analyze and forecast these interconnected factors. Yet, it has become clear at this juncture that IT has a preeminent role in how the world is connected. It will also steer the way forward in how industries practice interdependence while reducing co-dependence that contributed to a near stifling of the product and food supply chain for many industries with ties to China – the source of the coronavirus. Business as usual (BAU) will be re-defined in the post-COVID-19 environment where the crisis has exposed weaknesses and gaps in business operations that will be filled by technology for those looking to emerge strong.

What does the increasing presence of IT mean for teleworking, videoconference, e-commerce, and distance learning? As industries pivot to greater use of technology, more investment will be required in cloud services that store data and allows employees to access applications and platforms that manage workflow. From a small enterprise to large corporations, Amazon, Google, and Microsoft Azure are examples of computing services that will be used to keep people connected via servers that can store information, create information, and connect employees through a secure network.

Boom! That is the explosion that is occurring in e-commerce. More than likely, you, like I, have become a part of what is driving the train of accelerating revenues in this sector. According to the COVID-19 Commerce Insight studies, consumers are becoming more comfort-able with shopping online versus traveling to brick and mortar stores to purchase goods. From groceries to books people are shopping online and utilizing e-commerce as a way to purchase products and goods that are delivered directly to their door or food that is prepared for pickup. This pandemic has accelerated the shift from in-store shopping to online purchasing with revenues growing globally and reaching 146% growth in all on-line retail orders just for Canada and the United States during April.

Utilizing e-commerce platforms work synonymously with online businesses leverage that benefits from software applications that allow them to manage their website, marketing, sales, and operations virtually. Some of the leaders in the industry are:

- BigCommerce
- Shopify
- 3dcart
- WooCommerce
- Volusion
- Prestashop
- Weebly
- Squarespace
- Magento
- Wix

Many of these e-commerce companies work in tandem with digital commerce providers to process online money payments, with Pay-Pal having the strongest brand awareness. Competitors like Apple and Google have followed suit to create their platforms in the online money marketplace. Yet, the options continue to grow with players like Payoneer, Inc. that focuses on online shopping and Stripe which tar-gets online businesses as their primary customers.

The expansion of technology into various sectors will continue with healthcare seeing a rise in telehealth, which contains a broad range of services non-clinical services delivered remotely that may include health-related education. Technology is used to store-and-forward imaging or videoconference with health professionals to discuss health situations. It differs from telemedicine that involves remote clinical services. The World Health Organization describes telemedicine as an essential service in "strengthening the health system's response to COVID-19." In a world of social distancing, Telehealthcare services and telemedicine offers connectivity to health professionals in various locations without the need for face-to-face contact to address particular issues. Teladoc Health uses an integrated platform to connect its members to healthcare providers by collaborating with insurers, employers, hospitals, and healthcare systems around the world to provide virtual care. These are strong examples that answer all the questions in the four-way breakaway model that can be utilized for various businesses.

1

Leveraging Social Media

As the demand grows for consumers to remain connected to businesses, technology emerges to the forefront as a means to bridge the gap. Companies are using social technology like Facebook to conduct site visits. Utilizing social media websites like Facebook could also reduce the cost to place traditional advertising. Smart marketing exploits such opportunities knowing that people are spending more time on social media platforms increasing the probability of your Ad being seen and converting over new customers. The trajectory for incorporating virtual and social media platforms into corporate strategy is on the rise. Developing an online strategy means examining your company's current state and then determining what will be your message and your impact. Here are some important questions to ask:

- What does your company's current online presence say to customers?

- Does your company have an easy-to-use online interface?

- How much has your company invested in online marketing?

- What type of advertising campaign works best for your organization?

- Does your current website provide a quality user experience? If not, what changes are needed?

- Do customers experience an easy to use e-commerce process to place orders for goods and services?

- What percentage of revenue would you like to generate through online positioning?

- What methods are in place for customers to connect with the company via your website?

- Does your organization possess a reliable Internet provider? If not, what is your backup plan?

The last question posed is crucial to your business should you decide to make technology a greater part of your business operations. While advances in technology are especially useful, always remember that these instruments are created by man which means that there is always a margin for error. I recently had a personal experience where I was to deliver a webinar for the members of the Human Resource Management Association of Jamaica (HRMAJ). Throughout the week I had experienced a break in my Internet service due to the provider having challenges with their system. On the day of the planned event, I still didn't have Internet connection. To cancel the event would be devastating especially since it was the organization's first time using a virtual platform to deliver a service to its members. Calling upon what I had been taught early from my mother, always have an A and a B plan. Thankfully, I was able to utilize a mobile Wi-Fi hotspot I purchased from my Internet provider's competitor. Being thoughtful and planning for a situation that will cause a break in your ability to deliver a product or service to customers is primary to the sustainability of your business.

Many companies continue to struggle with embracing technology as a regular part of their business operations. In other scenarios, lack of awareness and familiarity with platforms that are best for a company also prohibits growth. This will ultimately hurt scalability for organizations as IT becomes more integrated into the day-to-day functionality of human life. Therefore, access to the needs of the business and decide what will work best. Your organization can hire an external consultant to manage your needs or utilize an automated platform that coordinates and manages your technological needs.

2

Low Cost and Free Resources

The expense of adding technology platforms to a company's budget can be difficult and cost-prohibitive for a lot of companies trying to find their way through the current crisis. During times of uncertainty, larger companies understand the need to make allowances that keep customers committed to their brand while also attracting new users. Several companies are currently providing discounts and free services to help address businesses that have shrinking revenues. Cisco Webex extended its offer to a 90-day free trial license that can be used for up to 100 participants to participate in webinars. Spike offers free videoconferencing for free with no download or account necessary and others like MicrosoftMeet are offering competitive pricing plans. During the COVID-19 crisis, Zoom has emerged has the virtual meeting provider of choice free accounts for up to 100 participants to attend a 40-minute meeting.

Whether its online platforms that create environments for work production or virtual software created for meetings using videoconferencing technology, finding ways to integrate these systems will elevate and sustain business enterprises. Businesses that have designed their solutions around the use of cloud computing will find great potential that affirms their brand presence.

Corporations have even found great uses for phone applications that uniquely link service delivery with customers. Home Depot's solution: allowing customers to receive an email for on-line orders that has product pick up identification information. Upon arrival, customers park in the curbside pickup area, call the number provided in the email, or via text notification and receive goods at the store once showing identification.

The creative use is exponential with collaboration mechanisms available through companies like WhatsApp, Tango, Viber, and others that are designed to quickly create group chats and phone videoconferencing that make connecting simpler and faster.

*"We cannot become
what we want to be by
remaining what we are."*
– Max DePree

Chapter 4

Claim Your Seat at the Table

One day you woke up and the whole world changed. Now things are very strange. The world is dealing with people being unemployed, underemployed, and some are still working, but in unfamiliar territory. The global health pandemic snatched normalcy, affecting every person and touching every industry causing economic disruption that would put your best skills to test.

Yet, you sit in an extraordinary position. You are among those in a leadership role with key responsibility for helping to implement how the organization will adjust to meet its immediate objectives. You are the hitch pin, each day moving fluidly between executive leadership and a larger team of employees who action the company's new set of directives. Things are moving incredibly fast. Employees are disgruntled, confused, and emoting complaints repetitively as others grapple with a different set of burdens as they face being unemployed.

Meetings are happening twice as often. Decisions are being made on the fly. There is no playbook or standard operating procedures to guide this process as government mandates and company policies change by the week, and sometimes by the day. Pause, take a minute, and remove your hand from the panic button.

Life is yet another term for 'keep moving forward.' The challenge comes when a shift occurs that throws you off balance. Feelings of fear, panic, and a host of other negative emotions can quickly hold you captive. You become impatient with not being able to control the process. This is a difficult place to be because you question every aspect of your current experience, standing in this crisis, armed with limited or no answers. There should be some consolation in understanding that this situation is not personal. It is a global pandemic that has affected millions of people, and while we struggle with the notion of how we will pay bills or stay employed, people keep losing their lives. That helps to refocus and set the mind on managing things within your control.

Instead of fighting feelings of frustration, anxiety, and being overwhelmed - deal with them. Use them as energy transformed to move you forward. The strength needed to arrive at your next destination as you discover how you contribute to making things better for the organization and yourself. While it is true you are in the midst of a crisis, you still have control over situations more than you may know.

In any crisis, you have a choice:

Nihil facere. Take no action. Be still and be a spectator observing the movements of the day.

-or-

Carpe diem. Seize the moment. Recognize the incredible potential this has to be a defining moment in your career.

Throughout the book I have discussed when a crisis comes it is also when the best innovators rise to the surface. I shared how Uber emerged as a market dominator during the economic mortgage fall of 2008. But much of what will be discussed when looking back on the historical record of this pandemic will speak to the great moves made by companies and global organizations. Little attention and study are usually given to the integral role middle and senior-level leaders play in shaping and executing the company's new or adjusted vision. That is your job.

You must widen your lens to envision what will be required of you now and what will be different for you on the other side of COVID-19. In the present, your small skills will be magnified. You will be required to demonstrate the multitude of attributes that define a resonant leader leaning heavily on your Emotional Intelligence (EQ) skills. The bar must be raised where there is deep thought that goes into the deliberate actions you take to engage with team members, peers, and senior leadership. This time will delineate your ability to put into practice the leadership skills acquired and expected of you as a reflection of what you have asked of other team members. How you chose to manage the conditions that unfold throughout this global pandemic will be the epoch that defines the trajectory of your career.

1

Moving the Needle

As a business professional, you have spent years cultivating your career. Whether through your academic achievements or your ability to use your innate capabilities to climb the corporate ladder. You are among some of the fortunate people who continue to be employed.

You are a part of what helps to sustain some sense of sanity in the world of business and for the customers they serve. Yet, the pressures of being in this environment is something you have never encountered before. Difficult situations throughout your career have arisen and you've successfully made it through them all. But this situation is different. It is global with no handbook or standard operating procedures (SOP's) on how to proceed.

What is in place is the years of experience and training that you can draw on to pull from your toolbox that will help you innovate and find a way to be a significant part of your organization's path forward. That is the mindset you must use to move the needle.

This is a rare occasion. It's a time that will determine your future when you pay greater attention to both sides of the coin. The side where you play a critical role in helping the organization find its footing in the new ecosystem, and the other side of the coin where you determine how this will impact your career as you seek to acquire your seat at the table. It is not unusual that people with leadership roles, heads of departments, managers, or directors are at times absent from the decision-making table. It is definitive evidence that position does not always equate to power. Instead, influence and impact are a milestone on the road to earning your seat.

Hear is something that may come as a surprise. COVID-19 unlocked a latent chamber of skills for you. You are learning to pilot through the conditions of a global health pandemic, the economic downturn that is occurring at the rising crest of how the business will remodel itself around the world because of technology. This is all happening simultaneously. At one end, five generations of talent are moving in and out of the new ecosystem. At the other end is where you determine the effort that must be made to acquire your seat at the table. It is not unusual that people with leadership roles, heads of departments, managers, or directors are at times absent from the decision-making table. It is definitive evidence that positions do not always equate to power. Instead, influence and impact are milestones on the road to earning a seat. When you evaluate the dynamics of these factors and the immense contribution key decision makers at the table will have on shaping the future, the significance of you having a seat can be understood.

2

Getting to the D

The Decision-Making Table is occupied by individuals with strong business acumen. They possess a willingness to contribute, the capability to make a difference, and are trusted for their input on import-ant decisions for the business. Gaining trust is earned by taking proactive steps to find ways to participate in the growth process, tackling challenges and consistently producing beyond expectations.

Occupants of the table work across culture and between departments by using strategic management practices to eliminate pain points.

They are the "how-to" and "go-to" individuals within the company because they know how to link departmental objectives with company initiatives using data to realize a positive impact on the bottom line. To have a seat you should be:

- An eloquent communicator.

- Acutely aware of the breadth and depth of company operations and the impact of your area of work.

- Know how to engage in constructive conflict.

- Define the problem, offer a resolution, execute the solution.

- Become aligned with the vision and mission of the organization.

3

Branding Your Career

Most people dedicate a small amount of time to craft the career they want. More time is often spent on finding a job that results in a position that often does not exercise full potential. To build a career is to be purposeful in defining what you want your life to look like and what strategic decisions you are going to make to reach your destination. The process of getting there is a journey, but it requires continuous cultivation. What does that look like for you? How are you spending time during this disorder to bring order and direction to your professional life?

If I asked you to take a ride with me, the one question you would probably ask is "where are we going?" Planning the way forward for your career is the same. There should be a clearly defined goal.

A vision for your ultimate destination that has a specific timeline for achieving goals and reaching milestones that become possible because of consistent things practiced. Have you found your answer to the question, "What do you bring to the table?" Hopefully, it begins with:

- A strong sense of who you are and how you authentically contribute.

- The secure grounding of self will show up in everything and will draw the confidence and respect of your peers.

- Willingness to add value to generously share knowledge, skills, and key experiences to improve current conditions.

- Work proficiency. A commitment to excellence in accomplishing tasks and achieving goals.

- Shared traits. One of the hallmarks of leadership is possessing common value with those positive leaders seated at the table.

- Strong relationship building. This is the currency of business. They must be genuine and reciprocal.

- Desire to pay it forward. Become a great leader by helping others succeed.

- Ability to use your voice productively. L3: Listen. Learn. Lend your ideas to the conversation.

Earning a seat at the decision-making table is a process. Acquiring new skills helps to build experiences that can be used to develop your expertise. This becomes fertile ground for how you will now position yourself to make an impact in the COVID-19 environment.

Find innovative ways to demonstrate your knowledge and make a lasting impact that will raise your visibility and bolster your brand.

Give voice to your creativity. This is the best time to use your super-power. It is the extraordinary gift that only you possess that can be used to accomplish a specific outcome in the organization. Use it to become the company's problem solver by taking the initiative to lead and contribute to strategic designs. In my profession as a leadership development expert, my superpower is working with individuals to help them make the mind and behavioral changes that amplify their leadership capabilities. In the time of a crisis, organizations need people who are great at structuring and leading ERGs and finding solutions in chaos. Individuals who can provide objective data-driven input that helps drive decision making.

Demonstrate that you are a thought leader in the organization. Create a proposal that outlines how your specific team or department can play a critical role in seeing the organization through this economic storm. It is not enough to have discussions. In times of crises where leadership will seek quick, but sustainable answers, your ability to put strategic plans together that are results-driven can make a positive difference in how you are perceived as an expert or change agent in your organization. If opportunities in your particular sector are minimal then find other ways to be an influencer by lending support in important areas of the business. The goal is to innovate where possible, contribute when necessary.

To strengthen your professional brand, pursue external business opportunities. This will build your profile at your company. Participating in conferences as a speaker or as a workshop facilitator, expert advisor, and educator in a specialty area solidifies your position as a specialist in your industry. This level of exposure affirms your commitment to expand your industry knowledge. This attributes more value to your capabilities making it easier for your voice to be heard, and your input solicited when leadership is in the decision-making process. Other ways to position you as an SME are:

- Hold a key role in a trade association.

- Participate as a member on a board of an organization.

- Speak up in business meetings providing value-added information.

- Write for an industry publication.

- Publish meaningful content and articles on LinkedIn.

- Apply to facilitate a TedTalk.

- Speak at a business conference or moderate a panel discussion.

Possessing a seat at the decision-making table allows you to be a part of things under consideration that may affect you and your team's scope of work. It allows you to be at the top of the mountain with company leadership, instead of struggling to manage the directives that role down the hill. Respect is earned when delivering data-based information that tells the story of why the case you are making is important. This is even more significant during a crisis because every decision is crucial and must be calculated for the residual effect it will potentially have on the organization.

4

Forecasting

While the nature of business means dealing with the unpredictable situations, leaders must avoid operating in ambiguity and become agile, remaining equipped to respond to complex and volatile situations. Businesses with forward-thinking leadership have a competitive advantage and remain positioned to survive. In your leadership capacity, being responsive to current conditions while working to understand future conditions that may affect the vitality of the organization is critical.

The ability to leverage what is known to envision the best way forward will help combat potential challenges as well as identify sources of commercial growth as discussed in the blue ocean to fast second strategic approaches. Your organization needs a leader who possesses the ability to better predict the needs and wants of the global marketplace for it to be equipped to meet changing demands. Remaining agile and flexible is an asset to meeting challenges in the ambiguous ecosystem. In a race to create new work dynamics, use your newly acquired skills to help demolish existing mental models of how the organization operates, heralding the way forward to embrace new ways of thinking and acting so the organization can move forward to operate on a new plateau.

These are the building blocks for you to become an influencer in the organization. Your seat at the table has drawn near. Once you capture it, use it to further your career. Journal copious notes that capture the integral role you played throughout the pandemic. Prepare to clearly explain the process used to develop plans, techniques used to solve problems, and alignment strategies with colleagues.

This becomes your evidence-based case study for how you and your team help create a "new normal" for the company in the post-COVID-19 environment. This will also guide your future conversations during the performance review cycle. Use it as a foundation for future promotions, bonuses, or a pleasing raise, without having to ask for it. The positive side of you creating a passageway through this COVID-19 journey, is that it will always occupy good real estate on your resume.

*"Don't aspire to be the best
on the team.
Aspire to be the best for
the team."*

– Unknown Author

Chapter 5

Know Your Position and Play It With Strength

One of the most important reasons why this book is titled, *Three Sides of Every Crisis: Strategies to Sustain Business, Manage Your Career, and Take Care of You* is to address the side of the story that often goes untold. To give voice to individuals who work to sustain organizations, but who often get forgotten. Most of the news headlines speak predominantly about the conditions faced by corporations fighting to cauterize plummeting revenues or business leaders who are the chief strategists. Little attention is given to the employees who are continuing to go to work in industries all across the world, contributing to society's ability to continue to function. All of this is happening in the backdrop while people try to find a way to manage through daily updates of increasing coronavirus cases and lives lost. Some of those employees continue to work full-time schedules. But many others have had their work schedules drastically reduced, and some have lost their jobs.

The fact is that there are several groups of people having various experiences during this COVID-19 crisis. According to Gallup, 81% of full-time employees state that their lives have been disrupted. These are people who are working to cope and learn to operate by a vastly different set of rules that materialize each day. Employers addressing safety and health management concerns have moved more than 60% of the U.S. workforce to work from home status, Gallup reports. Mirror images of this situation show around the world with the numbers varying from country to country, but the condition is the same. It is a blessing to be able to maintain employment granting financial stability. Yet, there exist a multitude of circumstances in the backdrop that create distinct challenges.

Employees who still have a job show up daily walking blindly as they try to adapt to the formation of a "new" normal for business. They carry the responsibility of putting out fires, creating solutions, and providing support for the remaining cohort of employees who are working to maintain the infrastructure of their organizations. These are profound issues to tackle because there is no playbook for how to deal with these incredibly unique circumstances.

1

Blessed to be Present

For many people, change is a dirty little six-letter word. It can be a painful process of accepting the changes in your environment as you compete in a tug-of-war to keep things as they once were, slowing down your process of acceptance. Yet, the blessing is that you continue to work: a position, unlike many others who are desperately seeking answers on how to meet their most basic needs. That has to be the foremost thought that guides your daily practice. You must believe that everything you need to make it through this situation is already in your toolbox. Wherever gaps exist, you must take the opportunity to add to your current group of skills.

Some people believe in accidents that have no meaning. I choose to believe everything happens for a reason that reveals itself in time, and the season in which it is meant to occur.

Despite the normal flow of your daily living being disrupted, you are seated in a position to work at a higher level. The peculiar nature of this COVID-19 environment calls for extraordinary actions. Use this as an opportunity to distinguish yourself from your peers.

Being ordinary will take you anywhere. Choosing to do the extraordinary will take you where you want to be. In this period of uncertainty, operating by usual standards could also give a false sense of security. As companies continue to find their way in these unchartered waters, there is still the possibility of additional layoffs. When consulting with one of our company's clients, we advised them to take a phased approach to downsize staff. This process would allow them time to work on a strategic plan that could be adjusted as changes in the environment occurred. Taking this approach would also mean they were able to retain as many employees as possible. The company's sustainability would remain intact as the organization found its footing. Lags in the supply chain and decreasing customer demand would mean the company had to enter phase two, where the second round of employees then would separate from the company. There is no doubt that this is an unpredictable period.

You must manage the things you can control, and one of them is the impact you have at work. There is no time to become stagnant. Get radical! Stretch yourself! Give more profound thought to the mere fact that you are amongst those who are gainfully employed. What can you do to help keep it that way? What can you do to turn this into a bold opportunity? Decide that you will take action to become an outstanding team player who practices collaborative leadership. Many people in the workforce have a misconception that leadership happens by acquiring a position or title. Leadership is a behavior. It resonates through your character and behaviors learned and actions taken over a period that enables you to adapt positively to the circumstances and people around you.

Get started by putting in the work to understand the vision, mission, and values of the company. Figure out what problems need to be solved and if you can be a part of creating those solutions. Employees often resist extending themselves when there is no guarantee of a positive outcome. That makes no sense because the evidence of you strengthening your skills and practicing leadership behaviors are assets carried with you forever. You can even debate the longstanding argument that the cup half empty or have full. It is best to recognize that there is plenty in the cup, and you have a responsibility to use what is accessible. Failing to take advantage of the opportunity is the difference between working a job and building a career.

2

Play to Your Strengths

Start with gaining a deep understanding of yourself and conclude with how you add value to the organization. Determine what are your strongest skills and your greatest assets? Ask yourself the question, "how do I use my (<u>strengths</u>) to deliver (<u>a specific outcome</u>) that brings value to the organization?" The answer to this question is crucial because it guides your mental outlook and governs your behaviors in the workplace. At the onset, answering that may appear to be challenging. That is because you have now decided to take ownership of your professional life in a strategic way that plots a specific course. It is time, right now, to grab the stillness of this moment to alter the trajectory of your life and retain control of the things that are within your reach. Make the first step by doing what comes naturally to you.

Then, decide to extend yourself to do something that stretches you to develop a new skill set and serves to encourage others around you. Write it down. Make your plan visible and put it in a place that you pass daily. Let your visual aide serve as a reminder of where you are headed while remaining encouraging about the things you can control. Work on them weekly. Do something that promotes goodwill and increase productivity as they collectively help move you toward your ultimate goal of making yourself essential to the business. So, where do you start?

- Ask your supervisor what assistance might be needed.

- Offer a solution to a problem. If you engage with customers regularly there must be an experience you have encountered that can help improve a process or resolve a problem.

- Be the team member that provides weekly updates in team meetings or WhatsApp chap groups showing the positive sides of the crisis.

- Provide support or assistance to a coworker.

- Share your knowledge. Hoarding information hurts the team and stunts your growth.

- Share weekly puzzles, mind benders, or motivational quotes.

- Deal with negativity by not participating when it shows up.

- Arrive to work early, not just on-time.

- Volunteer to be a part of or create a "vibes" team that facilities positive activities for team members.

Harness strengths that can contribute to the goodness of the organization and help you to reach your highest potential. If you are not sure what those are, seek input from family and colleagues or take an online assessment like Strength Finders 2.0 or Reflected Best-Self Exercise to understand your greatest attributes better. Maximizing your talent or the combination of several strengths you possess could result in management seeing you differently.

Individuals focused on a building career take responsibility to demonstrate how they contribute, instead of waiting to be asked by a supervisor or manager. Once you gain a complete understanding of your strengths, your value, and what problems you can help the company solve, it will create a clearer picture of your role in the organization. Your diligence and persistence can help improve relationships with team members and leaders as you work to stand out in the organization.

The steps you take now are essential for three main reasons:

- Personal commitment to reinvest in your professional development.

- Strengthen your workplace image and contributions.

- Evidence of how you productively used your time to find new opportunities during the crisis.

The constructive steps you engage in today will positively influence how to interact with your team members, meet professional targets, and provide greater fulfillment and enjoyment in both your personal and professional life.

3

Working Remotely

The tremendous effect the coronavirus pandemic is changing how work is performed. Employees are learning to adapt to new work structures while still meeting production demands. Both can prove exciting and challenging. For many years, the concept of remote work was not appealing to most employers. Many companies struggled to understand how they could effectively monitor employee performance and still reach high levels of productivity.

When introduced to employees, many embraced the concept of virtual work; thereby, welcoming the notion of having greater flexibility, saving on transportation, and the convenience of working in a comfortable space. The transition brings on a different level of mental and emotional adjustments that also require a higher level of discipline to work independently. Statistics have shown that employees work from home more because there are no longer chances to congregate with team members, eat in lunchrooms, or at area restaurants, and other attention grabbers. Many people struggle to create a private space and structured schedule, often suffering from boredom due to lowered in-person engagement with team members.

To win at remote work situation, review your work style, and create a process that you can commit to daily.

- Identify a private space in your home that is quiet and conducive for conducting professional business.

- Protect your space by including loved ones in the establishment of guidelines and ground rules for interruptions.

- Do a trial run to access peak activity hours in your neighborhood for potential noise and distractions.

- Check your technology – keep equipment charged, set everything up the night before a workday and have a plan B. Keep access to a mobile WiFi or hotspot available. Jazz up your workspace making it comfortable.

- Maintain a regular morning routine that includes breakfast and an early start to your workday.

- Respect company remote work policies and procedures.

- Communicate with your supervisor/manager twice as much than normal.

- Set, clarify, and maintain expectations around work productivity and timelines.

- Take scheduled breaks setting your alarm to keep you on schedule.

- Incorporate as much physical activity as possible in between work to stretch, walk, etc.

- Maintain work boundaries to avoid burnout experienced from working excessively and ease of availability.

- Be cautious to avoid becoming overly dependent on text, email, and direct messaging because intent, tone, and interpretations of-ten get lost in translation.

- Maintain high work ethics that mirror office professional behaviors of prompt responsiveness, timely availability, and collaboration with team members.

- Determine what brings you joy and helps you relax. Access them regularly to fight off boredom, loneliness, and stagnant feelings.

The world of work is evolving at a rapid pace. The coronavirus pandemic slowed down the economy while increasing the need to master adaptability. In this current state, organizations will need an employee who possesses the emotional maturity to work through the frustrations that this change has created and remain productive. Accept that things are different. Embrace realistic optimism that recognizes the hurdles, jumps them, staying focused on achieving results. Now go for it!

"Dreams have always expanded our understanding of reality by challenging our boundaries of the real, of the possible."

– Henry Reed

Chapter 6

It's Only a Dream Because You Let It Be

Every day people go to sleep resting on faith that tomorrow will bring favorable conditions that will help better the way they live. During the waking hours, the efforts you make bear down strongly on the results achieved. So, when adverse, disruptive situations occur through no effort of your own, being able to understand and deal with, it can be hard for many people. It just does not seem fair. It reminds me of the early lessons my mother taught me when she said, "when did I ever tell you that life was fair?" Wow, that was a profound moment. As a young person at the time, that was a tough concept to understand. In school, you are taught to play fair. Therefore, it seems natural to transfer that lesson into things experienced in life. But when shift-happens – when things change and that change is exceptionally drastic having no resemblance of fairness, it can be hard to cope. Accept that things are different. Embrace realistic optimism recognizing the hurdles, jump them, staying focused on achieving results. Now go for it!

The extremity of this crisis with its rapid debilitating health effects and the residual economic fallout undeniably caused a shock to the human system. The rippling waves of sickness and death to business closures and job losses hit with a force that caused the mind and the body to want to reject its brutal reality. That is certainly reasonable. It makes sense that you would experience a delay in accepting this new state of affairs. But when this season passes and you review the historical record of what you did to alter the trajectory of your life, make it a good story to tell. In his infamous poem, "Mother to Son" the Poet Langston Hughes wrote:

Well, son, I'll tell you:
Life for me ain't been no crystal stair.
It's had tacks in it,
And splinters,
And boards torn up,
And places with no carpet on the floor --
Bare.
But all the time
I' se been a-climbin' on,
And reachin' landin's,
And turnin' corners,
And sometimes goin' in the dark
Where there ain't been no light.
So boy, don't you turn back.
Don't you set down on the steps
'Cause you finds it's kinder hard.

Don't you fall now --
For I 'se still goin', honey,
I' se still climbin',
And life for me ain't been no crystal stair.

That literary work was written nearly a century ago with its most prolific message found in the closing stanza that beckons you to charge forward into the light of tomorrow - climbing and reaching out for fresh prospects, renewed perspective, and a zeal to endeavor toward greatness.

Your "shift" has happened. Job loss, being furloughed or laid off, will take you through the cycles of grief, "SARAH" that we discussed in the opening. Here is the start to you being able to heal, and to get the help that will put you back in control. Grab hold, manage your emotions, putting your energy into the pursuit of prospects that light your fire and give you hope. Focus on what you can control. Tackle your most significant pain points first. You have thought about it. You have dreamed about it. Now you can do something about it. It is time to run swiftly and strategically toward your ideal career.

1

Get Financially Fit

Reach out to your creditors to negotiate different repayment terms. This global pandemic is affecting everyone, so manage your responsibility to communicate about your situation to get the help needed. Consider getting help with credit and money management from organizations like Operation Hope. Reduce your spending as much as possible and use your savings for critical expenses. Adjust your budget to make essential changes. Explore government programs like the US unemployment benefits and the stimulus package. Jamaica established the SET Cash program to help laid-off or terminated employees who earn below the income tax threshold of JMD$1.5 million (US$11,127). Look for grants and other awards that offer assistance through private funders and non-profit organizations. Research entities like Nerd Wallet and FindHelp that list various ways to get assistance.

2

Adjust Your Sails

Time to find your silver lining in the dark COVID-19 cloud. Just as the pandemic created hardships, it also birthed a need for new services. Visit a job board or recruiting website, a theme emerges that shows job openings in various industries that are available in:

- Commercial cleaning services

- Food delivery

- Grocery stores

- Online learning companies

- Pharmacies

- Shipping and delivery businesses

- Tech support

- Virtual communication companies

Others focus on differing needs that are community-based for tutors or childcare. The website, TheMuse, provides information about jobs and companies and has explicit information on 87 companies still hiring during the COVID-19 crisis. Likewise, CareerBuilder states that jobs currently in demand with the highest growth are:

- Customer service

- Delivery drivers

- Doctors

- Grocery store employees

- Truck drivers

- Logistics

- Nurses

- Sales

- Time to update your Curriculum Vitae (CV)

You have skills, knowledge, and experience that have carried you this far. Draw upon them to guide you to your next destination. The current job market is ripe with opportunities for specific industries that continue to hire, as noted in the list above. Your CV should address each job opportunity, contain short blocks of text that are easy to read, and free of grammatical errors and should not include a photo. Write a creative and impactful profile opening statement and align it with your skills and experience outlined in the job description criteria. Highlight qualifications like Continuing Professional Development (CPD), certifications, and awards. If you include life experiences, tie them to essentials like budgeting and project management skills. Utilize a professional template or secure help from someone who specializes in writing curriculum vitae or resumes. It is a wise investment because it is the first impression potential employers will have of you.

3

Online tools

Utilize job boards and recruiting websites where you can register, post your information, and receive alerts for job openings. Maximize the power of LinkedIn's job search tools that allows recruiters to see your profiles. If you are uncertain how to organize your page, review profiles that are similar for the job you are targeting. Post a professional picture. Be sure to clean up your public social media presence mindful of the information posted on pages that you have marked as private that still can be accessed. Search for a website that helps with work reentry, job search, or career shifts like iRelaunch.

The virtual world has so much to offer. Today's reality also means learning and embracing several different platforms that will require you to participate in assessments, presentations, and interviews. Sharpen your skills now because every area that you can strengthen will distinguish you from others seeking the same opportunity.

4

Extend Your Learning

I believe in the power of mentors. While living in Savannah, Georgia, I met some beautiful people. Charlena and Charlie Brown were business owners who worked on political campaigns and assisted young, budding entrepreneurs. Charlie always told stories that would make you laugh and would leave you with a thought-provoking lesson. The one that impressed me the most is, "the mind is like a parachute; it only works if its open." A great reminder that learning is a continuous process, and self-improvement always adds value. The constant advancement in technology is a call to enhance your digital skills. This time is excellent to pursue one of your keen interest where time now presents a chance to explore it. Online courses are available for all fields from prominent schools like Harvard University offering free classes and Udemy has loads of on-demand video content representing a wide spectrum of courses. Increase your knowledge to enhance your personal growth and enhance your CV. If the timing is right, go back to school to pursue your next advanced degree or certification in preparation for climbing to the next level in your career.

5

Polish Your Expertise

> *"An investment in knowledge (skill), pays the best interest."*
>
> – Benjamin Franklin

This crisis has created a rare occasion where much of the world has a considerable amount of downtime available. Use this period to strengthen your existing skills and to perfect a technique. Practice and refine curriculum, become proficient in administering the assessment, master a technical skill, or revisit an area where you have a learning curve like social media tools, Microsoft Excel, or data analytics. There is always something in life that requires more attention or needs improvement. Check out free courses in subjects that range from language to robotics at ClassCentral.

6

Cast your Net to Get Work – Network and "Click"

Now, more than ever, people are coming to understand the power of creating an authentic relationship with people within your network. During an interview with Forbes magazine, George Fraser said while networking is a purposeful activity it can be selfish, requiring efforts to genuinely connect, or "clicking," brings higher achievement through values-based, mutually beneficial relationships that allow where people share common ground. "Clicking" is about creating chemistry, fit, and timing that align to build lasting and meaningful relationships. Value can be seen in bonds that are present and ready to celebrate in times of victory, and there to support in times of struggle. Authentic relationships for in your network mean that you have an open the door to reach out for advice, references, referrals, job leads, encouragement, and to elicit constructive feedback – the list is long. Those same connections, who care about your wellbeing, will be the first to lend help. This kinship is reinforced by you providing the same, so that there is a constant transfer of information sharing, connecting, and bonding that leaves both glasses full.

7

Date Your Next Employer

You have placed yourself in the job market, expressing that you are seeking new possibilities. Take a proactive approach to find the opportunities that meet your criteria. Think about when companies try to fill a position, they diligently assess the role and create a detailed job description that will attract the ideal candidate. As a job seeker, you should do the same. Make time to research companies to understand their corporate culture, work dynamics, salaries, benefits, and other things that are important to you. The company is a good place to begin but also read about their civic activity in the news and employee feedback posted on professional websites comparable to Glassdoor and Great Place to Work. Visit the company's social media pages, ask industry association colleagues for their insight, and create your list of questions that, when answered, before or during an interview, make it an appealing place to work. If possible, do a physical site inspection to see if the conditions are comfortable, meet your needs, and practical for transportation or relocation.

8

Make a 4-8-12 Plan

During your period of transition, get creative. Work hard to occupy your time with constructive projects that keep you engaged and bring enjoyment as part of your short-term plan. Think of how you might be able to turn a hobby into a revenue generator while applying for jobs or completing interviews. The job hiring timeline can be a bit of a process that takes anywhere from four, eight to twelve weeks, so position yourself to fill that void. If you are a secret chef in the kitchen, do meal planning, family dinner deliveries, or online webinars on how to master a particular dish. Use ingenuity to create a side hustle that you enjoy but may not be your interest as a full-time job.

Other ways to generate revenue are:

- Online sales promotions for large companies.

- Task Rabbit run errands and complete odd jobs.

- Rent your car using Turo or HyreCar.

- Sell your photographs of Adobe Stock, Shutterstock; Snapped4u for event photos and Fotomoto.

- Sell from your website.

- Completing online surveys offered by companies like Survey Junkie and InboxDollars.

- Shop watch videos and search the web with Swagbucks.

- Complete tasks and share your thoughts about websites and apps on Usertesting.

- Participate in market research studies with Elevated Insights.

During this pandemic, notable designers to the neighborhood seamstress manufactured basic and fashionable masks that met a critical need for people that also generated much-needed revenue. Find your space to occupy. Look for remote and contract jobs that offer part-time, flex, and freelance roles on websites like Flexjobs. A void may be filled while working on your bigger plan or result in special projects that have short timelines that get extended based on your performance and your ability to demonstrate your value to the organization. It is a short-term strategy to reach a near-term goal as you work on your long-term plan.

9

Compare Job Opportunities

What a perfect time to look at what the world has to offer. Think about what best suits you and place no boundaries on your options. Make your list of what is most important to you and research what type of jobs and industries are best suited for you. Consider your work style, do you prefer to work in teams or independently, what kind of environment brings you peace, and fuels your creativity? Design what would be your ideal position. You have the flexibility to consider every single option that you find promising and might want to do for the next half of your professional life. The time you have now as a result of this crisis is a break from your hectic schedule, and static routines that allow you to focus on finding your "sweet spot." Remain open to lateral and mid-career change, job moves, or a different industry. Take time to comparison shop, dis-covering the best elements of your future position. When you can see the other side of a crisis, you find out that you have options - a very empowering space to occupy.

Even though the rules of the game have changed, there is still room for you to learn how to make them work for you. This situation is complex, with several different factors to consider that require you to analyze the facts to determine the best way forward. Resist the temptation to act in desperation to accept the first job offer without being diligent in exploring your options. If you have done this in the past, there is no need to repeat the same pattern. Be mindful of red flags, directing all your concerns on getting answers to your most critical questions. Trust yourself and have confidence in your capabilities and your worth. This way, you can land solidly with a plan designed to work correctly for you that identifies the right position, is the right company, under the right conditions.

10

From Dream to Reality

Many years ago, I had an invite to speak with a traveling women's empowerment conference called African American Women on Tour, better known as AAWOT. This opportunity was preceded by me being an attendee at the event. I became so moved by women of color, from all parts of life, coming together to share their expertise, lend support to one another; and empower each other to do better. At that time, AAWOT had come to Atlanta. I walked into a session facilitated by a woman named Joann Tolbert Yancy. She was an engaging presence with a resounding voice and a message that rattled me to my bones. Joann and I would become the best of friends, traveling as speakers to business conferences in the Caribbean and throughout the United States. Repeatedly her sessions would be packed to capacity with people seated elbow-to-elbow or standing against the walls. It was not long before every person rose to their feet listening to the bold voice of the southern Arkansas corporate woman turned entrepreneur. She made people wrestle with in their hearts and examine their minds in search of an answer to the question, *"What Dreams Are You Sitting On?"*

Ask yourself that same question. You will find yourself at a turning point in your life. You have wondered about starting a business for some time. You have waited for the crack in the door that would give way just wide enough to let you step out on faith, believing in yourself, trusting that there is more to your story than the pages currently showing in your book of life. Well, keep writing. This crisis is your game changer. You thought it was your troublemaker. Instead, it is your bend in the road that tenacious entrepreneurs take to realize their dreams. History has shown that people with strong feelings of self-efficacy double down, turning obstacles into fruitful opportunities.

11

Where to Start?

Choose a fantastic business idea that solves a problem for a group of people that brings joy and satisfaction to you. Get serious about studying the peaks and valleys of business ownership. It is a work journey that will bring you rewards; yet, challenge you to the depths of your ability. The difference is, instead of having a role, you get to write the entire script. There are so many people in my life who taught me the value of running the race not just to win, but to finish strong. It is like a marathon runner. They run several laps or prolonged distances over trails conserving enough energy to accelerate as they draw nearer to the finish line. The strategy is not to compete like a sprinter because the effort would be short-lived or an exhausted finish leaving no energy for the next race. My point is – be wise in your approach. Based on your business model, financial resources, and personal obligations, consider a slow to moderate start.

12

Freelance, Contractor, Consultant, and the Gig Economy

The freelancing market is booming. It is a $ 1.5 trillion dollar economy that has rapidly emerged as a tremendous competitor to the conventional workforce model, according to Quora. It may be how you start your business. Upwork and Freelancers Union research shows that almost 50% of millennial workers are freelancing, and by the year 2027, the majority of the U.S. workforce will turn into freelance. This model is attractive because it is a self-employment structure that offers the liberty to work on various projects, usually for short periods that price work by the hour, day, or project. Companies like 99Designs and People Per Hour are examples of how to freelance and for-hire work experiences. However, the repetition of sourcing work offers less financial stability in freelance work. Another popular platform is Fiverr, also a global website where skills from web decision to family heritage research can be purchased for fees starting at $5.00 for work completed within a specific time. The creative website Etsy also provides a forum for individual online shops for entrepreneurs selling pre-made goods or custom design items.

Contractors typically take on assignments for more extended periods of time with a specific company or smaller cluster of clients that is defined by a particular agreement outlining the provisions of materials or services for labor. Consultants differ in that they provide expert opinion, advice, or direct training for a client to quickly deliver results that spur grow, offer a plan, or give a solution. All of these fall under the umbrella of the Gig Economy, which is a labor market composed of self-employed contractors, freelancers, consultants, and others who work short-term contracts. They enjoy the flexibility of negotiated work terms, remuneration, work location, and independent selection of clients. They are responsible for paying all taxes on earned income, which is the net figure derived after deducting work-related expenses. It is imperative to note that there is a learning curve who must come to understand how to:

- Provide a quality product or service that meets a need and solves a problem.

- Create a compelling "elevator pitch" that is succinct and accurate to explain the services or products.

- Attract, retain, and grow clients and customers.

- Price goods and services.

- Develop a strong brand.

- Build and retain a resource network.

- Hire the right people.

- Sell what the business offers – USP (unique selling point).

- Create a marketing strategy.

- Grow the business.

- Commit to a succession plan.

- Create an exit strategy.

Enter with a mindset that failure is not an option. Recognize that operating a business parallels life in that it has highs and lows that are conquered when you anticipate and plan for hardships. The only way you fail is to ignore the lessons from your experiences. The pain of experience is that the lessons will continue to be taught until they are learned.

13

Traditional Business vs. Gig Economy

As I write this, I am excited about the generous upsides that you now have the chance to consider due to this crisis. The sheer effort you will put into these considerations will fill you with new knowledge and renewed hope that you will get through this situation armed with so much more information. That is encouraging.

Traditional businesses take on different structures like limited liability companies, small corporations, limited liability partnerships, and can be for-profit or not-for-profit entities. They have quite different tax classifications, requirements, and filings. As the Gig Economy grows, traditional businesses and larger companies are utilizing the services of the tenant of the Gig Economy because it offers access to:

- A highly skilled talent pool.

- Negotiated pricing.

- No payment of health, insurance, pension, or other benefits.

- On-demand, round-the-clock work accessible around the world.

- Better cost control of budgets.

- Scalability for rapidly changing projects and business growth.

The Gig Economy is a rapidly growing freelancing ecosystem composed of more than 62 million people in Europe and the United States, according to the McKinsey report, Independent Work: Choice, Necessity, and the Gig Economy. They categorize workers who:

- Get their primary income from actively pursuing independent work as agents.

- Use independent work to supplement their primary income and are called casual earners.

- Make money from independent work but prefer traditional jobs known as reluctants.

- The financially strapped, who do supplemental independent work out of necessity.

Independent workers generally fit into four segments.

Share of working-age population engaged in independent work

	Primary income	Supplemental income
Preferred choice	Free agents 30% | 49 million	Casual earners 40% | 64 million
Out of necessity	Reluctants 14% | 23 million	Financially strapped 16% | 26 million

Source: 2016 McKinsey Global Institute survey of 8000 US and European respondents
McKinsey&Company

Both Traditional Businesses and the Gig Economy are financial living organisms that are morphing in response to the global transformation of needs and demands expressed by the five generations of consumers and technological advances that influence the pace of change. The business start-up climate has adjusted its sails again amid the coronavirus pandemic. The crisis has presented new challenges that might make starting a business a bit of a timid idea. History shows us it is just the opposite. Economic downturns are gateways to "tremendous opportunities for market disruption," states Entrepreneur magazine. The way forward for business is adaptability and flexibility that will make way for the coming tide of change to present something new, align itself with complementing what exists, or emerge from among the crowded space to be a secondary entrant that dominates.

Based on the current state of business transformation and slowed economic growth, here are ten recommendations for start-up businesses with a low financial investment are:

- Cleaning Services

- Culinary Coach

- Creative Content Developers – graphic designers, website, Social Media Influencer

- Educational Tutorial Services – a virtual platform

- Horticulturist

- Online Courses and Training

- Life Coach

- Delivery and Shipping Services – Amazon, UPS, and others

- Smartphone Repair

- Social Media Management

There is no shortage of information or resources you now have at your disposal. Trust yourself to know that you are going through a time of transition with abundance waiting on the other side. Begin crafting the masterpiece to shows how well you conquered the unpredictability of this situation and made it work in your favor. If doubt tries to find its way to you, as my good friend Ebuni always says, "life is a journey, not a destination." Be thankful for the time granted to examine areas of your life where positive changes can be made that would have gone unaddressed under normal conditions. Do not become stagnant in the use of your gifts.

Chapter 7

Healthy Living in a Covid-19 Environment

There is so much joy to experience when you can find hidden blessings in unexpected places. This crisis has undoubtedly been one of those cases. The world is finding new ways to manage the mental and physical effects that has brought abrupt changes to our daily routines. Millions of people have been forced to quarantine at home with spouses, children, significant others, and some alone. It created room to re-examine what is healthy living. More time now is being spent cooking meals at home, finding ways to fend off weight gain, and ensuring that the right attention is being given to your mental wellbeing. The New York Times described it as being in a "dual crisis of mental and physical health," citing the Kaiser Family poll, where more than half of the respondents said the coronavirus had harmed their mental health. While this may be valid, we cannot get stuck in that place.

Now, more than ever, taking care of your mental and physical health has to be a major priority. People living with preexisting psychological conditions and those with health issues will have their experience exacerbated by social distancing orders, significant shifts in diet, and reduced access to healthcare services. For some, this is a battle, and for others, it is a war – both have to be won. After thumbing through the pages of this book, you know my answer is having a positive perspective and making a conscious effort to find the goodness in what masks itself as feeling like hell.

That means self-care has to be a priority for your psychological, social, emotional, and mental wellbeing. When you implement the right strategies, it will increase your body's defenses against lots of pathogens, including bacteria and viruses. There are plenty areas to take a look at, starting with stress.

1

Eliminate stress triggers

Chronic stress depresses the immune system and increases the risk of various types of diseases. When being subjected to extreme amounts of stress, the level of catecholamines increases in your body, causing an adrenaline rush that triggers feelings of fright. These factors affect the amygdala of the brain inhibiting short-term memory, the ability to concentrate and retain long-term memories, which the health website Very Well Mind says prolonged exposure is harmful to your health. There was a period during my workaholic life where not a year would pass without me getting sick with a cold at least two or more times. The high degree of stress made me more susceptible to viral diseases, especially respiratory illnesses like the flu and cold. Thank goodness I tackled that years before this epidemic. Proper stress management is essential to combat the coronavirus and to avoid triggering other health problems. Finding an outlet that brings you back to the center and makes you feel some excitement, joy, or release is the goal. Find your peace by practicing mindfulness, yoga relaxation techniques, getting lost in a mystery novel or adult coloring book to find your peace.

2

Keep a positive attitude

Expect good things, and your immune system will follow. Be optimistic. Try to see the glass as half full, not half empty. Practice gratitude and think of at least three things that you are grateful for every day. Imagine the best result for situations, even difficult ones. You may not always be able to control the events around you, but you can still decide how to respond to them. Respond with an excellent attitude to in-crease your chances of getting the best result and strengthening your immunity.

3

Power up Antioxidants and Minerals

Increase your antioxidants to help remove potentially harmful oxidizing agents. You can find antioxidants like vitamin C and E in fruits and vegetables. These antioxidants are compounds that protect against free radicals. When you take antioxidants, it improves your immunity and overall health. Eat foods like melon, kiwi, oranges, broccoli, berries, carrots, watermelon, and green leafy vegetables to enjoy these benefits to your cells and immune system. Dr. Geoffrey Mount Varner, an emergency room physician and expert consultant on how to make split-second decisions has been hosting Facebook live medical information updates sharing that Vitamin D consumption is really important to fight the coronavirus. Darker-skinned African Americans have less Vitamin D which means they need additional amounts which can be found in fatty fish, beef liver, cheese, and egg yolks that have this mineral. And, of course, basking in the sunshine helps.

Minerals like magnesium, selenium, and zinc also help in improving the function of your immune system. Meals with more vegetables, fruits, and lean proteins and probiotics may also help says WebMD. Expand your grocery list to include yogurt and fermented foods, like kimchi and sauerkraut.

4

Probiotic supplements

Some research suggests that the compounds in herbs and supplements may improve immune systems. Some herbs that have immunostimulatory benefits are licorice, black cumin, green tea, ginseng, milk thistle, astragalus, and garlic. Get your best guidance from a pharmacist or a doctor before adding herbs and supplements to your regimen to ensure proper use and reduce potential side effects.

5

A word about comfort foods

Processed foods like snacks, fast food, soda, and candy can be comforting, but only brings temporary pleasure and can trigger longer adverse effects, like emotional eating. Comfort foods contain empty calories that do not give your body the necessary fiber, nutrients, or vitamins needed to boost your immune system. However, any food you enjoy can bring comfort. Healthy living is a balanced diet and avoiding anything done in excess.

6

Engage in indoor exercises

Exercise has numerous health benefits, including prevention against heart disease, osteoporosis, and others. Activity is also an immune booster. University of Virginia School of Medicine, Professor Zhen Yan says that the antioxidant EcSOD, "extracellular superoxide dismutase," can protect against acute lung disease and other diseases like ARDS (acute respiratory disease syndrome), which is deadly in 45% of the coronavirus cases. If you previously were not committed to a regular exercise regime, then making the transition can be uncomfortable be-cause of the strain on your muscles and skin. The good thing is that you have lots of options. If you struggle with the monotony of a routine, find creative ways to get 30 minutes or more of exercise in a few days of the week. Add variety, walk, dance, learn a new "step" dance, or join an online exercise group or take Debbie Allen's free Instagram live dance class. The necessity of adding exercise, whether it is squats, push-ups, sit-ups, or jogging in one spot for a while, improves both your mental and physical health. Along with a healthy mind and body, the physical results are great.

7

Do not cut down on sleep

Several studies confirm the link between sleep and a healthy immune system. Most people need 7 to 9 hours to feel adequately rested. Get-ting the right amount of sleep helps improve white blood cell function. With proper sleep, you are also less likely to get ill. To optimize your sleep, you need to adopt good sleeping practices. Try to avoid things that can interfere with your sleep like the consumption of alcohol and caffeine close to bedtime. According to experts, a cooler room helps you sleep better, and you can complement this with a relaxing nighttime routine. Whether it is a cup of tea, relaxing music, or a warm bath that you can do to assist with relaxation and to fall asleep more easily.

8

Maintain CDC cleanliness guidelines.

Frequent handwashing is a simple and effective way to prevent the spread of respiratory infections. Some germs are easily transmitted from person to person when we come in contact with each other. It's easy to transfer germs from your hands to your nose, eyes, and mouth if you touch them. This can make you sick. Wash your hands with soap under warm running water. Rub the front and the back of the hands as well as between the fingers. Antibacterial soap and hand sanitizer can provide additional protection against microorganisms. Use an alcohol-based hand sanitizer that contains at least 60% alcohol when you don't have access to soap and water.

Chapter 8

Beating Back Boredom

Here is a challenge. Find ways to combat boredom during this trying time while resisting the temptation to lounge excessively and become inactive. Ready. Set. Go. There have been many stages to the shelter-in-place orders. The first was the shock of it all, where boredom was not as great of an issue. Then, acceptance which has you looking for ways to maintain positive mental stimulation. Even keeping track of which day of the week can be tricky. Time starts to feel like it is yesterday, today, and tomorrow.

You may find yourself spiraling around lots of small, short term activities that become chains of things that continue to feed feelings of boredom. Even doing meaningful work that is too hard where you struggle to stay focused can be boring. The key is to do things that are meaningful and lasting as well as seeking out activities that have a purpose and that challenge you. Start with tapping into personal skills and talents to do things you find enjoyable. Knowing the difficulties so many people are facing because of the numerous way's life has interrupted, and even turned upside made me want to use my counseling and coaching skills to help others. I continue to be amazed by the power of just listening. Passing no judgment, allowing people to release negative emotions, and just giving them a safe space to be heard. It is not about giving advice. It is simply being present to walk part of the journey with someone who is struggling. Activities that provide purpose and that can be done continuously extend your vision beyond today and get you unstuck, so you abandon negative feelings and behaviors.

Here are seven principles to guide you through this time:

- Begin by guarding your thoughts. Reframe your thinking to help change your attitude about it.

- Do things that add value or teach you something new or make you feel good.

- Explore activities that are rewarding because they help others.

- If you prefer structure, create a regiment that helps you feel grounded in the routine you create.

- Go with the flow. There will be few times in life where you have time to be unstructured without certain consequences. Embrace the temporary freedom of a fluid lifestyle.

- Indulge in guilty pleasures – Binge on a television series and other hobbies, giving yourself permission to relax and enjoy.

- Stay connected. Feed your soul with love shared by videoconferencing with friends and family; attend service online to get spiritual nourishment; call on your mentors and become a mentee. The only way out of monotony is with others.

Now is the time to put to use your inventive mind. There are multiple ways to approach this situation, a positive outlook and positive actions yield a host of benefits. The barrage of craft projects, jokes, and TikTok videos have brought out talents that would have stayed hidden. It is also a chance to refocus with vision boards or Steve Harvey's ask God for 300 things challenge to help envision great possibilities. To get what you want out of this life, you have to be committed. Along the way, enjoy the process and take in the beauty around you. Begin right at your fingertips.

Here 20 Creative Ideas to inspire you:

1

Travel – Explore the World, Virtually

There is more than one way to travel. Sure, we can't visit the Great Wall of China or see a magnificent cathedral in Italy right now (at least physically), but there are other ways. I'm talking about virtual tours. There are lots of virtual fun and mind titillating things to do. You can take virtual tours of zoos, museums, art galleries and so much more. Due to the pandemic, lots of zoos are incorporating virtual tours into their websites. Here are some cool places to visit from the comfort of your homes:

- National Museum of African American History and Culture contains more than 35,000 treasured artifacts that tell the story of black history in America and the country's legacy of racial injustice. It will open your mind to the important ideas and themes preserved in this museum.

- Guggenheim Museum in New York takes you to the center of Frank Lloyd Wright's masterpiece surrounded by art collections and exhibitions that tell provocative stories. Visit the website or take the amazing virtual tour of the Guggenheim museum.

- National Museum of Modern and Contemporary Art, Seoul, South Korea: Add this one to your bucket list. In 1969 , it opened to capture South Korea's history, and has become the epicenter of the country's modern art.

- Van Gogh Museum, Amsterdam: For more than three decades, the Van Gogh Museum has been home to thousands of Vincent Van Gogh creations. Located in Amsterdam, it is one of the most visited museums as people marvel at the Dutch painter's Western art collection and stories of him severing part of his ear during an argument. Here is your chance to check out some of his most famous paintings, including "Self-portrait," which he made in 1888.

- National Museum of Anthropology, Mexico City: The National Museum of Anthropology, located in Mexico City, is home to what we would consider the world's most extensive collection of ancient Mexican art. In this museum, there is a massive collection of ethnographic objects and an undeniable testament to the preservation of the indigenous legacy and cultural heritage of the country. There are several items for you to see, and you can get more than a glimpse of the famous Aztec calendar sunstone thanks to their virtual tour.

- The Louvre: which usually needs a ticket to Paris before seeing the famous collection in the impressive art museum. To see the entire complex is a multi-day visit. Their outstanding exhibits, including the widely acknowledged Egyptian antiquities, can be seen during their free virtual tours.

- The Great Wall of China: One of the country's most famous tourist attractions that has a magnificent history that is tied to the country's economic development and cultural progress of the country while safeguarding trading routes such as the Silk Road, and securing the trans-mission of information in northern China. No matter where you are around the world, an excellent way to practice self-care during this trying time is to take a virtual hike on this wonder via their on-line tour.

- MARS: Why don't you take it a step further and visit another plan-et? Well, thanks to the virtual tour from NASA, you can visit MARS right from your living room. As long as you have an Internet connection. Get a taste of what scientists' experience on their expeditions. There is so much to learn on this tour, and of course, it won't be short on fun, especially if space exploration is one of your interest. On this tour, you can visit four locations, which constitute a significant part of NASA's Mars Science Laboratory mission. Explore the Pahrump Hills, Marias Pass, Murray Buttes, and Curiosity's landing site in style.

- Monterey Bay Aquarium: Animals are not left out. Thanks to the virtual tour from Monterey Bay Aquarium, you can admire and watch animals in their natural habitat live. A great indoor activity for families, children, and aquatic animal lovers.

2

Practice yoga

A great way to guard your physical health is to engage in an activity that is soothing to both your mind and soul. It helps you to keep calm and also takes at least 30 minutes off your day. That is 30 minutes of boredom eliminated, and yoga is beneficial to your physical and mental health. Start your morning meditating silently and reminisce on things that make you happy. Relax and breathe deeply to release feelings of anxiety, stress, and other negative emotions to help you stay in control of your emotions, and even improve the quality of your sleep.

3

Learn something new

Of course, you're not going to be building rockets or become an expert on navigating ships, but there are lots of other skills you could beef up on while you are stuck at home. One of the best parts about this is the generosity being shown by organizations that offer free online course. Check out the list provided earlier in the book. What are your major interests? What are some areas where you can improve? Here is an excellent time to reflect and learn more. If you are a lover of graphics, this is a great time to take a graphic design course. It is a major market-mover, and who knows, after a while it could be a source of income.

4

Revisit an old project

Do you have an old project hidden in the depths of your computer that you feel is not worthy of being published? Are there some activities you started up but abandoned because you were preoccupied by other things? Well, now is the time to dust them off and complete them.

5

Apply for grants and loans

Do you know that entrepreneurial opportunities are lurking and waiting for you to grab? Right now, loans are low, and it could be the perfect timing to finally get started on that dream you've been holding on to. Spend time checking the internet for awards, grants, and fellowships relevant to your field of study. Search deep, and you will find incredible treasures, although not all will be accepted. However, for every rejected grant application, you have learned something new about grant writing that will make the next one better.

6

Link up with other professionals

Many people are adjusting to working from home. While you are spending time isolated at home, this could be an excellent time to think about the next stage of your career. You can reach out to professionals who are currently in the field you are interested in and spend valuable time discussing their careers. Since physical contact is not advisable, you can do this via Skype, a phone call, or even via their social media pages. This way, you will be building your network from a distance and still planning for your future.

7

Have a steady routine

By maintaining a steady routine, you can be able to manage anxiety better and adapt quickly to the harsh reality. Even though you are working from home, let your routine incorporate both work and non-work hours. You should have that time of the day when you are working and also the time of the day when you are into other activities. When you are not working, engage in activities that bring you joy and make you forget, at least temporarily, that there is a virus running around. There are also advantages to working in short bursts. It will help with productivity as you won't get burnt out and will have a more transparent train of thought.

8

Show compassion toward others

It is a tough time for all of us, more for some than others. Extending compassion towards others is a win-win for both parties. You can call those who are lonely around this time and spend time sharing words of positivity. You will discover that talking to others is a powerful buffer against amplifying feelings of distress. We know we can't be our best selves all the time, but we can reach out to others to offer help when needed.

9

Maintain virtual connections with others

Even the most introverted of us need a sense of connection with others for our mental and physical health. Many working groups have created virtual forums where you can contribute or just sit back and enjoy the conversation. Work teams have designed virtual café groups, on-line book clubs, and collaboration workspaces to connect, learn, and share. We are in social isolation, but there are ways to avoid feeling lonely.

10

Get started on long movies or books

How about a little entertainment? Movies are an excellent way to pass the time, especially as they offer a lot of intrigue and suspense for those who love a fantastic storyline. From horror and romance to action and thrillers, there are tons of movies available online to catch up on. A lot of us didn't have time for movies before the coronavirus, and now you can experience these stories again. Take in a docuseries and do a watch party with family and friends. If you are not much of a movie lover, then dust off some bestsellers from your bookshelves and indulge in them during this isolation. Either way, these will eliminate the feelings of boredom.

11

Learn a new language or refresh an existing one

I can hear the wheels turning, and you are wondering how. It is not impossible to do, and there are apps to help you on this journey. Imagine coming out of isolation with two new languages in your arsenal. You can do a quick search online to find the best app that is compatible with your mode of learning, and before you know it, you have learned a new language. Dedicate at least an hour each day to your classes and take it as seriously as if you were getting a degree.

12

Puzzles and board games

I know that technology has stopped most of us from engaging in physical games, but there are other ways to connect. Some people download an online version then get physical. However, who says you can't do both? Get some puzzles and board games and have some fun. Download games like the Words with Friends App and have a family faceoff. If you are isolating with your family and miss those afar, this is an excellent time to boost your family connection.

13

Volunteer at a non-profit

Alternatively, you can spend this time making a massive difference in the world. Not only will it help you stay active, but you will be impacting the lives of hundreds of people positively. So, check for any non-profits locally that would need your help and offer support by helping with Virtual administrative tasks, updating their website, planning post COVID-19 activities, and more. If there is none locally, you can expand your search to other organizations.

14

Self-reflection

Take time for some self-reflection. Evaluate your life thoroughly and try to list out things you have to change. Check out the positive aspects of your life and list out those things you should continue doing. I call it walking through your "beautiful ugliness." Life can get so busy that it becomes a process of ideas and exchanges, leaving little time to evaluate the best and not-so-lovely parts of yourself. It is time to take responsibility for where you are currently in your life, with a mission to affirm your current position or recalibrate to get better aligned to reach your goals. Treat this time as a gift of two-plus months of downtime to refresh and retool. To emerge from this time, having no productive outcome would be a lost opportunity.

15

Bake or cook something special

Grab your goodies or get them delivered from grocery stores, independent supermarkets, farmers, or farmer's markets. Even better, this time has inspired people to grow gardens to have a personal organic food supply. Challenge yourself to cook a full course meal with appetizer and dessert at least once a week.

One thing I have come to love is cooking something from a different country every Sunday. If you have never attempted baking before, now is an excellent time to start learning. Who knows, you might enjoy it so much that it becomes a regular thing even after when the pandemic is over. It has become a bit of a competition between my mother, daughter, and I, with the winner judged on the quality of her presentation.

16

Start an indoor garden

It may sound surprising, but one of the most effective ways to practice self-care is to take care of something other than yourself. With that in mind, this could be the perfect opportunity to start an indoor garden. Start your plant journey by contacting your local plant store to find out what type of vegetation will work best in your home, and if the store delivers. For those of us who don't have patios or a lawn to escape to while still socially estranged, taking care of plants will be especially rewarding.

17

Start a craft project

In the past, have you been mad at the question "what are your hobbies?" simply because you don't have time to do anything by yourself? Well, now you may have the bandwidth to choose a hobby, and why not look at the arts and crafts field? Find a small craft supply store in your area and shop for everything you will need to create a master-piece - think of yarn and knitting needles, needle or paint kits, and canvases. If you are nervous about starting a new creative project, use the store as a resource by visiting their website where loads of ideas are posted. One of the best things about small businesses is that those who work in them are almost always extremely passionate about their area of expertise. They will likely have advice on where to start.

18

Eliminate that word boredom and replace it with a blessing.

Many things are good and have the potential to be even better. Taking the time to connect with others, get to know your loved ones more, and reassessing your next set of life steps is powerful. Embrace the opportunity.

19

Adopt a pet

There are many benefits to having pets, and boosting your immune system is one of them. The Centers for Disease Control and Prevention says that having pets has been found to decrease cholesterol levels and also lower blood pressure. When compared to those who do not have pets, pet owners usually have lower triglycerides and cholesterol. This tip could translate into a lower risk of heart disease and overall better heart health. Even better, pets are excellent social companions that can help you exercise and prompt you to go outdoors.

20

Harness the power of your social network

The growing evidence from many studies suggests that loneliness and social isolation are very harmful to health. In one study, those with the strongest social relationships were more likely to live longer than those with poor social connections. Harvard Medical School found that strong social relationships decreased depression and reduced the risk of premature death by 50%. There are many ways to develop and strengthen social ties. Pick up the phone and call your friends more regularly. Join an online class or group related to your interest or hobby you have. Keep up with old friends and make new ones to strengthen and expand your social circle. Do a family videoconference call to connect with loved ones all around the globe.

Chapter 9

Minding Your Mind Matters Most

It is easy to feel extremely uneasy with all the uncertainty going around, and that is why a significant part of self-care involves, not neglecting your mental health. Every decision you make, even who you choose to not take action, is a decision that flows for the positive or negative condition of your mind. Your thinking process impacts your emotional, physical and spiritual states which can cause great feelings of being in control of your life or the opposite. Protecting your thought process and keeping your mind strong is primal to good mental health. Take steps to ensure that you don't compromise on your mental wellbeing. Affirm what is positive and remain grounded in that space. Give yourself permission to work on turning weaknesses into strengths and making your strengths stronger.

1

Personal Development

You can manage your mental health by focusing on personal development. I came across a Personal Development Bucket List for Self-Improvement by Ell. The contents are perfect for this. Not all of them can be done during isolation, but eventually, we know that we will come out of this situation. At some point, it will be safe enough to get out and start working on getting our lives back to normal. However, during this time, there will be new challenges which you will have to adjust to, which are potentially stressful. Extract parts of the list that you can start on while you are at home and complete them when you can. This bucket list is detailed and will keep your mind refreshed.

Listed below are a hundred ideas for the development of your bucket list. However, you need also to incorporate discipline while developing your list. Make sure that you have a set time frame for each, checking them off as you move on to accomplish the next one. You can personalize this list by being specific on what success means to you. Setting personal goals that are significant, meaningful, and purpose driven. You can also input a reward system by tracking your overall improvement and treating yourself to something special after an essential milestone. Discover ways to stay motivated and committed to your development. Remember, this is a journey, not a destination. Take each item one step at a time and be sure to enjoy the process of becoming a better version of yourself using Ell's Personal Development Bucket List:

- Attend a personal development workshop.
- Attend a personal development retreat or seminar.
- Get a mentor or coach.

- Learn how to meditate.

- Learn about mindfulness.

- Do one thing every day that scares you (no matter how big or small!).

- Take part in a meaningful volunteer program.

- Set up and run your non-profit project.

- Focus on developing your self-confidence.

- Learn all about self-love.

- Complete a 30-day challenge of your choice (if you wanted to, you could tie this into your development bucket list and tackle one small one, each day, for 30 days!).

- Complete a 365-day challenge of your choice.

- Get into the habit of waking up an hour earlier than you usually would.

- Stand up and speak to a group of people.

- Stand on a stage and speak to hundreds or thousands.

- Take on a fitness challenge that will test your physical and (more importantly) mental strength.

- Conquer a fear – like a skydive if your fear is for heights.

- Learn a new language, well enough that you can speak it fluently.

- Start a journal – because a life worth living is worth recording!

- Learn to say "no" without feeling guilty.

- Learn to say "yes" to more things that will push you outside your comfort zone.

- Overcome your anxiety.

- Know how to deal with depression.

- Speak to a therapist about something that's always troubled you.

- Start studying something new, just for fun!

Let's Keep Working Through…

- Break a bad habit. It could be smoking, drinking, excessive eating.
- Develop an existing strength or talent to become more of an 'expert.'
- Learn all about body language and what yours says about you.
- Set a goal for the number of books you'll read in a year.
- Set a goal for the number of audiobooks you'll listen to in a year.
- Learn how to better manage stress.
- Learn how to work more productively.
- Identify both your strengths and your weaknesses.
- Work on improving one of your biggest weaknesses.
- Get into the habit of writing a Gratitude List every morning.
- Commit to life-long learning, developing in a new area every month.
- Do a little solo traveling.
- Live in a different country for a month.
- Learn about different religions and how they live.
- Deprive yourself of five 'luxury items' for a week.
- Learn about Body Confidence and become happy in your skin.
- Learn the art and power of forgiveness.
- Stay single for at least a year.
- Don't use any electronics for a week (yep, this includes your phone and the TV!).
- Donate an organ, or if not – at least give blood.
- Do something you always told yourself you couldn't do
- Volunteer at a homeless shelter on Christmas Day.
- Visit the elderly to help tackle loneliness.
- Get clear on your values.
- Define your life purpose.

We're Halfway There – That's Our First 50!

- Write three things every day that you want to achieve… and achieve them.

- Improve your communication skills.

- Learn to let go of any pain of the past.

- Don't say anything negative for an entire day… or even try for a week!

- Set something up within the community.

- Do something good for nature – like litter picking, a beach clean, up-cycling.

- Campaign for something you're passionate about.

- Create a self-improvement plan, starting… now!

- Do more acts of kindness with no expectations for anything in re-turn.

- Take time to get to know yourself.

- Destroy the habit of procrastination.

- Become a better, more active listener.

- Play more strategy games, like chess or Othello.

- Take a self-defense class.

- Develop a growth mindset.

- Don't be afraid to say what you think. Practice speaking up more!

- Get clear on what happiness means to you.

- Learn how to prioritize.

- Build an online community of like-minded people.

- Nurture optimism.

- Learn a new hobby – perhaps to sing, play an instrument, or dance.

- Stick to a New Year's Resolution… for an entire year!

- Cut toxic people out of your life.

- Work on improving your leadership skills.

- Learn how to invest.

Into Our Final Quarter...

- Master your habits.

- Help in a third-world country.

- Increase your exercise and develop a new weekly routine.

- Attend a yoga or Pilates class.

- Learn about affirmations and positive self-talk.

- Define your vision of success.

- Create a vision board for your life.

- Learn about your mind, emotions, and how to manage them better.

- Learn about diet & nutrition, vouching to cook more, and eat healthier.

- Take a new online class or course.

- Practice self-care and establishing a better work-life balance.

- Increase your daily water intake to hydrate your body and mind!

- Develop mindful journaling.

- Create a new, inspiring workspace.

- Identify any things that are holding you back... then work on them!

- Develop the habit of writing daily to-do lists.

- Speak to ten new people who inspire you.

- Make new friends with like-minded people.

- Start a new side-business.

- Use timeboxing to work more efficiently.

- Reduce the amount of time you spend on social media.

- Heal your negative self-talk.

- Join a mastermind group.

- Watch a personal development video or Ted Talk every single day.

- Set goals... and then even bigger goals! You've got this, trust me!

2

Staying updated with happenings

I have to admit, initially I found myself glued to the news about the coronavirus. This is common with almost everyone. We are trying to latch on to any piece of information we can find about the virus, but this can lead to anxiety. If you find yourself waking up each day to check the number of global deaths from COVID-19 or staying up to date on the various myths and propaganda being peddled about the origin of the virus, then you need to take several steps back. Refrain from checking out unverified reports that can only lead to panic. So, here is a suggestion, limit the amount of time you spend listening to the news and focus more on staying safe. When getting information use reputable sources that tell you the latest methods of protecting yourself and your loved ones.

3

Keep your mind active

Having an active mind is vital for your mental health. So, even if you are not with your family, engage in a lot of jigsaw puzzles and brain teasers. They require critical thinking to solve them, and even crossword puzzles can be fun. Do what is necessary to help you get through this tough time. Just a few minutes of solving puzzles gives your brain the needed action to distract you from what is happening. Be careful about how much time you spend watching the news. Curtail the easy access to 24-hour access to news as well as the amount of negative information you take in from social media. Most importantly, do not rely on one source for information. Be diligent in checking credible resources that provide a balanced view.

4

Stay connected with family and friends

It doesn't matter if your family members or loved ones are far away. Distance shouldn't be a barrier. Spend valuable time talking to your family either through video calls or voice calls. Your conversations shouldn't focus too much on dire happenings. Instead, try to share laughs and talk about happy moments as much as you can. Share how much you love yourselves and let that joy radiate around you. With this, you will be able to maintain positive thoughts that there are people who care about you. Check-in on friends as well, talk about those fun moments you shared.

5

Be in the moment

Pay attention to physical sensations around you by being mindful of the present. Consciously let go of negative or stressful thoughts about the occurrences around you, which can weigh you down. When you are participating in your routine activities like eating or taking a shower, bring awareness. Don't get lost in thoughts, and if your mind does wander, be sure to get back to the present. A right way of ensuring this is to listen to soothing music. It doesn't have to be slow and sad songs all the time, even songs with a beat that you love will help brighten your mood.

6

Be mindful of the company you keep

Pay closer attention to your network, to ensure that the people you are communicating with are nourishing you with the information needed, to positively feed your mind. Strike a balance, so you avoid spending much of your time with people who find nothing positive to share or who do not wish to add value to your life. Your circle of influence should be broad in range enough that it encompasses people who are smarter than you. If you are the smartest person in your group, find a new group because you are not learning. Some find this harsh because they misunderstand the concept. You can maintain friendships, but to grow, you have to learn from others. Adding to your circle enables you to continue nourishing what exists while inviting more into your life.

7

Don't be afraid to get help

There are times when this feels too heavy, too tough, and it is perfectly okay. Be gentle on yourself. Part of coping is the last step in the SARAH process – heal and get help. You must do this in the form that works best for you. It takes a lot of courage and will to maintain good mental health with the threat of a deadly virus hovering around. Now that our lives have been disrupted suddenly, with most of us having to stay away from work and school, we no longer have access to many things that were significant factors in our daily lives. When it feels overwhelming, and you think you are starting to sink, don't hesitate to seek help. Seeking support is a sign of strength, not weakness. Use dedicated hotlines in your communities where you can talk to a professional who can listen to your concerns and provide the necessary resources.

Apple offers a COVID Coach, a free app that connects you to resources for coping and adapting to the Covid-19 pandemic. You don't have to do it all on your own, and there is always help if you are willing to accept it.

Chapter 10

Navigating the Next, New Normal

"When peril or crisis pulls your trigger, whatever explodes depends on what you are loaded with."

Dr. Frederick D. Haynes, III

On a cold day in March, I was sitting in a crowded room in a sea of red and white, sharing space amongst the women of Delta Sigma Theta Sorority, Incorporated. Like me, who had come from Jamaica, we had assembled from all around the United States and the world to converge in Washington D.C. It was Social Justice Sunday, the spiritual celebration that is part of the annual Delta Days in the Nation's Capital (DDNC). We sat, ate, and shared in conversations about the activities taking place throughout the week, looking forward to the speaker, Dr. Frederick "Freddie" Haynes who would take to the podium to deliver a message unlike any I had ever experienced. He laid out the context of his speech, wrapping it around facts, numbers and examples that personified his powerful and impactful message. It was like watching a master quilter weave the pieces that would materialize into a signature collections item that would hand in a museum. He spoke so eloquently that the entire room erupted, rising to their feet, letting out roaring affirmation and excitement underscoring his prophetic and powerful message. While writing this book I came across Dr. Haynes again. This time he was sharing a quote that I used to open this chapter. In essence, its meaning says to me whatever exists within the composition of your being will find its way to the surface when pressured such that greatness will rise or weakness will cause things to tumble.

The shock and awe that this crisis has created are understandable. However, it is part of life's reformations that require you to make the necessary adjustments. Depending on how you choose to change your perception about this experience will determine how well you embrace the next "new normal." Yes, the next "new normal" because things will never be as they once were. And, normal is relative. The reality is that different circumstances create refined ways of doing things. The world has discovered areas of commonality and need that previously went unnoticed. Bonds have been created; broken fences have been mended. New relationships have formed; some restored, and others have ended. Systems have been tested, dismantled, and reconstructed. Economies have been pressured, depressed, and they will be restructured. It is the changing of seasons that will place each of us in the mode of learning how to adapt and adopt new practices in a post-coronavirus environment.

Businesses that were recipients of government funding to help cushion the casualties in the private sector will see regulation or attempts to nationalize specific industries to ensure positive dividends from those financial investments. Consumer expectations may rise as a result of the funds derived from taxpayer dollars and demands for companies to release data that show how funds are being used to maintain jobs and return-to-work plan for employees.

How countries will cover the cost of stimulus injections into the economy will more than likely result in increased taxes. Collectively this may result in a stressed economic system that will influence weaken consumer buying power and that will stall an upswing of economic recovery for industries like fashion, travel, and others.

Another significant shift will be the increased use of on technology and automation. People have begun to use technology more often to manage communications using platforms like Zoom to access healthcare information utilizing Telehealthcare systems, and for transportation and logistics to manage the supply chain using robots and driver-free 18-wheeler vehicles that move goods across the country. These factors will strengthen global connectivity and accelerate efforts to meet consumer supply and demand. However, it will also create a society where more jobs leave the market. The McKinsey Global Institute predicts 400 million to 800 million jobs by 2030 will potentially be affected by automation. These changes will stretch people to rethink the most basic interactions of human contact.

The global race to find a vaccine for coronavirus means that social distancing will be a regular standard practice for some time. The impact on businesses will differ based on industry and the means of survival pursued during the crisis. For example, the healthcare system in the United States will undergo a major examination of how medical care systems can be better integrate national systems and create a network for controlled, universal access to data. The travel and hospitality industry will have to reimagine things like spaces that limit contact and allow for quicker transactional purchasing. Food services that will see a pendulum swing from luxury dining to convenient pick-up and delivery.

Companies will have to invest in training team members on how to manage disruption through strategic and critical thinking models that still allow for creativity. Leaders will need to take a comprehensive approach to manage a blended workforce of in-office and remote working, which will become a permanent fixture. Virtual work will also elicit new policies and compliance standards. It may even mean less brick and mortar facilities needed as the number of employees required to be inside buildings begins to decrease. Training employees on how to manage independent, no-contact environments, a dramatic shift requiring new ways to motivate and measure performance, will be necessary. There will be diversification of service and product offerings as companies seek to meet consumers' needs. The new world order will call for a smart balance of personal engagement and technology platforms in the workplace. With human contact changing, companies will need to spur innovation that increases personalization. Consumers will desire to feel significant and valued as a customer as the use of technology increases.

Whether your organization rises like a phoenix from this crisis will be a testament to how well your company invested in its team members, how committed your team is to the organization's vision and the actual relationship you have created, and manage to sustain with your customers. The commitment your team has to the organization will show up in the creative strategies formulated to help mitigate the challenges and risks faced in this crisis. Satisfied customers, especially those who had their expectations exceeded, always come back.

Microsoft founder Bill Gates said this crisis means dealing with an invisible enemy you can't confirm its presence because it is difficult to fight what you cannot see. The act of visioning is often navigating within the bowels of the unknown charting a course based on what information is available to map a way to the comfort of what will become what is probable and profitable. Here are some truths on how to do that:

- Recognize the pattern – disruption, restructuring, renewal.

- When the shift happens, visionaries adjust.

- Pay attention to the forces that may hinder business continuity and the effects that may create new opportunities (in every opposition there is an opportunity).

- Assist team members through the stages of SARAH.

- Leverage your global village of mentors, counselors, and consultants.

- Know your strengths, face your weaknesses.

- Embrace the Next, New Normal.

- Envision victory while celebrating small wins

- Create and ready your Plan B.

- Design your crisis management strategy.

Here comes the culture shift. The organization's identity will need to be firmly defined in an arena where its mission may be adjusted, and structure changed to accommodate new work models, customer and industry demands. Engagement will have to double along with communication and innovative inclusion of your workforce to help create the next "new normal". Together they will all fuel talent retention and acquisition that will need to make space for the Gig economy.

There will be many organizations that come out of this one top. During the recession of 2008, a study by Bain & Company found that twice as many companies did well moving from "laggards to leaders" in their particular industry during the downturn versus periods of economic calm. Getting there means paying attention to competitors, suppliers, and customers in your industry. Don't forget about the new entrants. Look toward the horizon and plan for reaching the summit.

- Consider what result you want on the other side of this crisis.

- Act now. No time to waste during these two-plus months of social distancing and self-quarantine.

- Decide what will be your story of opportunities pursued and gained.

Personal dynamics will change with individuals reassessing all things financial, technical, and those that are touchpoints. People will reassess how money is earned, spent, and saved leading them to become more conservative until the storms of the crisis become quiet. A fixture will be exploring multiple streams of income to manage a simpler lifestyle that is less strenuous in the light of the next disruption. We are far off from a debt-free economy, yet consideration toward managing and reducing debt will be an emphasis.

A new crop of crisis management leaders will emerge getting noticed for how well they were able to transition or head change management initiatives. Employees will also seek new opportunities in "recession-proof" industries and entrepreneurial ventures. As people are forced to reach outside their comfort zones to find ways to stay connected, greater emphasis will be on personal connectivity and nurturing relationships. The crisis affects everyone differently, with some conducting extreme makeovers changing the dynamics of how decisions are made to sustain relationships and grow careers.

Individuals will question and reaffirm the values and ways of exercising faith with new constructs for worship to be adopted. The changes in the way people fellowship will increase virtual religious service participants and programs. People will lavish in modified ways of interconnectivity with technology granting virtual access to various schools of thought and practices being readily accessible.

As people have more time away from the fast-paced demands of deadlines and duties, citizens will embrace an eased pace, moving away from frivolity and excess busyness will occur. The time spent away from work environments will continue to reshape how people define their work arrangements and increase the numbers of people exploring opportunities in the Gig Economy and other forms of alternative income streams. Companies will also be challenged to finds ways to connect with customers whose palettes have shifted to desire more personalization and sensitivity toward diversity that embraces cultural and demographic differences as strengths.

The flattening of the curve of this crisis will become applicable to various parts of how we all adjust to the next "new normal" way of living. People will learn to embrace disruption that will erupt at intervals affecting the growing globally diverse populations who will practice more interdependence exemplifying that we are indeed closer in our common needs, then we are apart in our individual desires. It is through these interactions that the greatest opportunities will be found to tackle perceived obstacles.

Epilogue

Here we are at the closing of this part of the journey. Landing in a place where there is full understanding that throughout life, comes difficulties. This time the magnanimous challenge came in the form a global health pandemic. Despite what often appears as being immensely overwhelming, the incredible gift is hidden in the spirit of human nature that fights to uncover the beauty that can come out of it.

When you consider the number of hardships experienced in life, the lesson has always been to gain the right perspective to find a positive outcome. It is fascinating the amount of energy we will put into all things negative. And yet we struggle to find the effort toward making our circumstances for the better. It is futile to spend excessive time fighting the current reality, only to fall deeper into a difficult situation where you participate in unproductive conversations that can only serve to make you feel worse? This book is your guide to finding the silver lining in the dark COVID-19 cloud. It is your playbook to rebuilding your business, taking ownership of your career so that you are not just working a job, with none of this being possible if you fail to take care of yourself.

After at least two months in quarantine, what will be your story of how you spent this time? This book helps you take a 360-degree look at how to find opportunities in a crisis looking through the lens of an entrepreneur, employee in a business, and then it gives you a wider-angle personal view. There is an immense sacrifice that goes into forming a business. Perhaps you are in the sunset of your company's existence and figuring your way through this disaster seemed as if there were no answers. I can only imagine the heaviness that may come with being a neophyte of business ownership, and then out of nowhere, here comes this gigantic wave. Within every entrepreneur lies the restless the spirit of a warrior. That is what drove you to chase the dream. The battle may be tough, but you cannot surrender without giving it the best fight ever. There were plenty of stories shared in this book about the brilliance of new emergents during an economic crisis like Uber and the brilliance of a tenacious spirit that brought us the mobile phone. As a business owner who has gotten knocked down a few times, it made me want to work even harder. And I did. So, will you. When your victory comes, the stories you will be able to tell becomes a part of your arsenal. The team that powered the company through this season helps you to recognize their essential value more intimately in maintaining your company's success and sustainability. A crisis reaffirms that your best idea may have struck the match to start the business; however, it only burns bright because of the team that continuously works to keep the vision alive. Together, you can move between the hills and valleys much easier. When you recognize the value of this experience, you will have elevated your business acumen such that you will deal more efficiently with future challenges finding your way to new opportunities faster. Embrace the hike up the mountain because the lessons learnt make the scenery on high even more beautiful.

Times like this make you take pause. Evaluate how you have been contributing to the world. Examine the energy you have been putting into the construction of your career. Turn off the news channel that only gives you one side of what seems to be only side of an ugly story. There is no benefit in that for you. Choose to feed your mind with information that will help you find the unlocked door. Find person, a mentor or coach who will share with you what you need to get unstuck and aligned to a different way of thinking and behaving.

The second side of this crisis seeks to send a wakeup call, sounding the alarm to address the decisions employees make to have a job or nurture a career. The world is not the problem; it's me and you. The way we interpret the disruptions in life and how decisions are made to create a roadmap for the future. If this pandemic taught us anything, it was that complacency will always keep you trapped from fulfilling your greatest potential. This period was the needed tap on the shoulder that made you look at the strategic place of your life. Maybe it revealed that you are moving along well, giving a reminder not to get comfortable and to keep adding value to how you show up at work. For some, it provided greater focus to using your gifts to turn a difficult situation into a dream that has been long suppressed. In the entertainment world, when a show goes live, they say "this is no dress rehearsal." I employ you to rise from this with a renewed commitment to take greater control over working in excellence to cultivate a career that reflects the best of what you have to offer the world.

This crisis is a huge megaphone shouting that it is no longer acceptable to show up and work just to collect a check. Think about this: you spend more time at work than you do with the spouse or partner you love; the children you raise; the neighbors in your community; even with yourself. Work is where you spend the majority of your time. It makes sense that you work a plan that exhibits the best of your gifts and talents. Think about every purchase you make represents the affinity you have for what that brand offers, like the quality and dependability of Mercedes Benz and the sweet, thirst-quenching taste of Coca-Cola products. How you engage in the workplace becomes the building blocks of your brand that exemplify the value and significance of your brand that exemplify he value and significance of your contributions. Choose to work differently. Because deciding to make no changes is a passive aggressive act that surrenders your power to winds of life's ever-changing cycles. Changing your perspective is a proactive step toward having influence and impact over your destiny. The way you participate becomes the diary of your greatest professional achievements and a reflection of your self-worth.

Stay woke! That is what the coronavirus did for everyone. A call to action to remain continuously aware of the changes in and around you. It is a balance of regular self-evaluation while discerning the external forces' that tap and pull on your life. This is the most critical side of looking at the crisis. Why? None of this matters if you fail to get yourself right. To triumph in business and bask in a great career centers on your positive and productive holistic well-being. I gave this the closing attention, so it would be that which you remember last. A strong, sound mind that is at peace with the decisions you make drives the train to maintain a healthy body and to feed a soul filled with joy. Apple Inventor and Co-founder Steve Jobs taught us that there is no amount of money, professional accolade, or personal achievement that is better than living a healthy life. He amassed a billion-dollar fortune and shared some profound words as life came to a close, Jobs said he had reached "the pinnacle of success in the business world" that was the epitome of success in the eyes of most people only to realize his immense pride in becoming wealthy.

He added they stop here without no substation for being able to live a life that should cherish where they eat good food as medicine, rest, exercise, spend time with loved ones, and an expound on enjoying the human experience. It is a reminder to take care of the one body and on life given, not allowing the weight of any situation to snatch your resonance. Grasp the opportunities before becoming relentless to walk in the blessings of this process.

The best that will come as you surface from this crisis is that you will have invested in creating a better life for yourself having evidence of time well spent, despite the distractions and disruptions that tried to take you off course. I will say it again, there is irony in this crisis coming from China, a country whose belief system says that danger and opportunity are on the opposite sides of a crisis." Decide where you will spend your energy. Remember that,

"Your beliefs become your thoughts,
Your thoughts become your words,
Your words become your actions,
Your actions become your habits,
Your habits become your values,
Your values become your destiny. "
Therefore: Keep all your actions positive

- Unknown author

Afterword

Action Three Sides of Every Crisis

1. Visit Jewel Daniels Websites

- Book and Speaker Website: www.jeweldaniels.net

- Corporate Website: www.dcleadershiptraining.com

2. Attend a Free Webinar

Participate in weekly 45-minute webinars focused on topics relevant to entrepreneurs and business professionals.

3. Schedule an Event

Arrange to have Jewel be a speaker or facilitate a workshop for your company, organization event or conference. Send an email to connect@jeweldaniels.net or call 876.546.5020.

4. Connect with Us on Social Media

LinkedIn: www.linkedin.com/in/jeweldaniels

Facebook: www.facebook.com/Jeweldanielsspeaks

Instagram: www.instagram.com/jeweldanielsradford

Twitter: https://twitter.com/determined2lead

Copyright Notice

About The Author

Jewel Daniels is a passionate and engaging corporate trainer, speaker, and entrepreneur who has built a global business with a client list that includes the US Army, Couples Resorts, Vistaprint, Megamart and the City of Savannah, among others. She is the author of three previous books, *It Takes Tenacity, 15 Power Moves to Survive the Wilderness and Weather the Economic Storm;* and *The Enterprising Entrepreneur* and *Growing Solopreneur Business Through Collaboration.*

Jewel has been featured in various publications like Skirt magazine, Onyx Woman, Georgia Trend magazine, and The Savannah Morning News and has received recognition from former Georgia Gov. Roy Barnes and Congressman Jack Kingston.

She holds a master's degree in Organizational Leadership degree from Capella University and was the first African American woman accept-ed to Seoul, Korea's Yonsei University where she studied International Relations and Political Science. A proud Hampton University alumna and graduate of New York University's Public

Relations Institute, Jewel has a tenacious spirit for learning and developing leaders. She has also served as an Adjunct Instructor at Savannah Technical College and Armstrong Atlantic State University and is a trained Stephen Minister.

Serving in professional organizations, Jewel is the president of the Human Resource Management Association of Jamaica Western Chapter, and president of Delta Sigma Theta Sorority, Incorporated Jamaica Alumnae Chapter. She has also served as the past president of Association for Training and Development Savannah GIG and member of the Montego Bay Chamber of Commerce. She is a community service advocate having served on the boards of Communities in Schools, the MLK Foundation, and Quantum, Inc.

She is passionate about her work, loves to read, travel, and paint. Jewel enjoys mentoring young women and believes that her greatest gift is her daughter Jynnah, a social anthropologist.